ALTERNATIVE
TO INTERVENTION

A World Peace Foundation Study

ALTERNATIVE TO INTERVENTION

A New U.S.-Latin American Security Relationship

edited by

Richard J. Bloomfield
Gregory F. Treverton

Lynne Rienner Publishers · Boulder & London

Published in the United States of America in 1990 by
Lynne Rienner Publishers, Inc.
1800 30th Street, Boulder, Colorado 80301

and in the United Kingdom by
Lynne Rienner Publishers, Inc.
3 Henrietta Street, Covent Garden, London WC2E 8LU

Library of Congress Cataloging-in-Publication Data
Alternative to intervention: a new U.S.-Latin American security relationship / edited by Richard
    J. Bloomfield and Gregory F. Treverton.
    Papers from four several-day meetings in the United States and Latin America organized by
the World Peace Foundation.
    Includes bibliographical references and indexes.
    ISBN 1-55587-217-4 (alk. paper)
    1. United States—Foreign relations—Latin America—Congresses.
2. Latin America—Foreign relations—United States—Congresses.
3. Latin America—Politics and government—1948-   —Congresses.
4. United States—National security—Congresses. 5. Latin America—National
security—Congresses. 6. United States—Military policy—Congresses. I. Bloomfield, Richard J.
II. Treverton, Gregory F. III. World Peace Foundation.
F1418.A543 1990
327.7308—dc20
                                      90-36326
                                          CIP

British Cataloguing in Publication Data
A Cataloguing in Publication record for this book
is available from the British Library.

Printed and bound in the United States of America

The paper used in this publication meets the requirements
of the American National Standard for Permanence of
Paper for Printed Library Materials Z39.48-1984.

Contents

Preface

In the decade of the 1980s, Central America, long a backwater of U.S. policy, suddenly became the subject of intense and often vindictive debate that ranged from the halls of Congress to the op-ed pages, from academe to the town meeting. Yet, U.S. intervention in Latin America was nothing new: it was an issue that had plagued U.S.–Latin American relations since early in this century. Previous efforts between the United States and Latin America to resolve the problem had not been fruitful. The Organization of American States, which was created after World War II to seek collective solutions to security crises in the hemisphere and thus to avoid unilateral intervention by the United States, had been ineffective in the Central American conflict.

The World Peace Foundation decided that it was time to look beyond the immediate question of Central America, to examine the reasons for the failure of the existing collective security machinery and, more important, to see whether U.S.–Latin American cooperation on security could be revived. Accordingly, the foundation, with its own resources supplemented by grants from the Ford, MacArthur, and Rockefeller foundations, launched the study project that resulted in this book. At the end of the study, the participants, who came from many nations in the hemisphere, issued a statement, included here as an appendix.

While recent events in Eastern Europe should remove some of the motives that gave rise to intervention in the recent past, a reading of the history of U.S.–Latin American relations shows that the problem of intervention predated the Cold War. The hope of the study participants is that it will not survive the Cold War.

The editors wish to thank their patient authors and others who contributed to the effort: for organizing the series of successful meetings of the study group, Stephen Brager and Margaret Kourbetis; and for proofreading and other chores, Elizabeth Umlas and Paul Laurino. Our special thanks go to Theresa Baranski, who, with skill and dedication, coordinated the exacting job of preparing the manuscript for publication.

Richard J. Bloomfield
Gregory F. Treverton

Introduction

Gregory F. Treverton

This book is the product of an intriguing effort in problem solving organized by the World Peace Foundation in Boston. Several dozen participants from the United States, Canada, Latin America, and the Caribbean worked through cases and concepts in four several-day meetings in the United States and Latin America. We met enough to get to know each other and to become frank. It was an unusual collaboration.

We addressed a single question: can the United States and Latin America break out of the cycle of insecurity, fear, and intervention into which they seem locked? The prospect or fact of revolutionary, Marxist-Leninist regimes in Latin America invokes security concerns in the United States. Whatever their own concerns about the regime, the Latin American states quickly come to worry more over the risk that the United States will intervene militarily. The Latin Americans seem more worried about the U.S. response than the threat, convincing the United States that it must act alone. And so Latin America gets what it fears most: a U.S. intervention. So it was in Grenada.

So it was, more recently, in Panama. Mikhail Gorbachev and change in the Soviet Union may mean that Marxist-Leninist regimes in Latin America are fewer and less likely to evoke security concerns in the United States. But impulses to intervention will not go away. New issues like narcotics provide one set, old issues in new forms, like promoting democracy in the hemisphere, another. All risk repititions of the same cycle in relations between the United States and Latin America.

In seeking to reshape collective security in the hemisphere, we focused on purposes, not institutions. We shared the premise that there are institutions aplenty. Ours was no mission to revive the Organization of American States (OAS) or other of the formal inter-American machinery. If those institutions have a role to play, and they may, all to the good; if not, they can remain in obscurity. In any case, our inquiry was how the security interests of both the United States and Latin America could be met without intervention.

1

Defining Intervention

International law defines "intervention" as "dictatorial interference in the affairs of another state for the purpose of altering the actual condition of things."[1] Even by that definition, the word "dictatorial" leaves plenty of room to argue over what is and what is not "intervention." Latin Americans often have construed intervention broadly; any form of "interference" is tantamount to intervention.

During the 1930s, U.S. policy distinguished between nonintervention and noninterference, and sought to reflect both. Not only would the United States not intervene in Latin America directly with military force, it would also refrain from using its influence to insist that changes of government be the result of elections that could be labeled "democratic."

However, nations affect each other's politics in so many ways that any too-tidy definition of "intervention" is suspect. They decide whether or not to grant other states economic aid and whether to assist them in getting loans. Even if these decisions toward other countries are not explicitly political, the decisions in any case have political effects on the country in question; of that fact, foreign political leaders have no doubt.

The definition of "intervention" becomes fuzzier still in considering other state actions that do have explicit political purposes. Many nations beam radio programs at each other; the aim is public information for political purpose. The West German political party foundations receive grants from the government. They spend money on political and labor organizing on behalf of sister parties in the developing world. Those party foundations set the model for the U.S. National Endowment for Democracy.

In our conversations and in this book, we held to a narrow definition of "intervention," one that would be accepted by almost everyone. Here, it is the use of military force, whether openly acknowledged or not, to affect the "actual condition of things,"—that is, the domestic politics—of another country.

Assessing the Failure of the Inter-American System

The inter-American collective security system constructed after World War II—the Rio Treaty of 1947 and the OAS established the next year—were based on the principles of nonintervention and collective security. All sides agree the system failed: it failed to prevent both the conditions in Latin America that impelled the United States toward intervention and the interventions themselves. Understanding that past failure is the task of the first three chapters of this book.

James Kurth and Heraldo Muñoz explain the failure in similar terms despite writing from different national perspectives: the structure could not reconcile the conflicting perceptions of national security held by the United States, on the one hand, and the nations of Latin America, on the other. For the United States, as Kurth points out, the structure, like its predecessors, was driven more by extrahemispheric than by inter-American purposes. It was "not so much inter-American as anti-European," intended to prevent the expansion of the major European powers into the Americas.

In American eyes, the bargain was that Latin American states would make common front with the United States against an extrahemispheric threat and, in return, the United States would protect smaller Latin American states against aggression by their larger neighbors. The problem was that cases of clear-cut aggression in Latin America, ones that would induce small powers to accept American help, have been relatively rare.

In the harder cases, when Latin Americans perceived the threat as internal but the United States as external, the system could work only if both agreed the external was the source of the internal. The instances for which that was the case, Cuba and the Dominican Republic in the 1960s, represent for Kurth the high points of the system from the U.S. perspective. Latin Americans feared internal unrest and saw it as inspired in part by the Cuban revolution. And the United States was making good on an implicit plank in the bargain—providing economic assistance through the Alliance for Progress.

According to Kurth, this conjunction of circumstances collapsed by the 1970s. In South America, regimes had turned repressive, and economic flows had become private, unconnected to any bargain over security. The system was irrelevant to the security challenges of the 1980s—from conventional war in the south Atlantic between Argentina and Britain to revolutionary war in Central America.

Muñoz agrees, but he would say that the system's high points were such only for the United States: "the system provided security for the United States but produced insecurity for Latin America." The system was based on two myths, a Western Hemisphere ideal and the equality of the region's states. Moreover, Latin America expected the system not only to provide economic assistance comparable to the Marshall Plan but also to entail a U.S. commitment to nonintervention. It was disappointed on both counts.

Broader changes in the international environment, Muñoz argues, also opened new possibilities for Latin American states, such as the emergence of new powers in the region, the recuperation of Europe and Japan, and the breaking down of the East-West antagonism. At the same time, Latin Americans tried new forms of cooperation among themselves—the Andean Pact for instance. In sum, by the late 1970s the United States had much less control in the region than it had in the late 1940s. It could enforce its notion of security no longer.

Jorge Domínguez demonstrates the clash of security perspectives by comparing U.S. approaches to two Latin American revolutions two decades apart—Cuba and Nicaragua. He emphasizes that the U.S. interest in keeping European powers out of the Americas was not merely strategic, it was also ideological from the start. President Monroe opposed not merely European influence; he opposed their systems as well. That ideological element was sharpened by Wilson, muted by Franklin Roosevelt under the pressure of strategic necessity, and reemerged again in opposition to communism.

In responding to the Cuban revolution in the 1960s, the United States achieved its objectives save one: the Castro regime did not fall. Cuba was "isolated, punished and condemned. In the process, the inter-American system failed to work as a mediator . . . and became, instead, an alliance against one of its founders, whose regime and policies had changed unacceptably for the other members." While the United States and the Latin Americans initially differed in responding to Cuba, they soon converged, before diverging again in the 1970s.

By the time of the Nicaraguan revolution, the inter-American system had ceased to exist; on this point, Domínguez agrees with Kurth and Muñoz. He emphasizes one more recent blow, the effect of the south Atlantic war. Latin Americans (and many U.S. citizens as well) simply did not believe the U.S. government's diagnosis of, or prescription for, Nicaragua. Nicaragua was different from Cuba in important respects: it was less important economically and more plural politically.

On the other hand, Nicaragua, like Cuba, sought to export its revolution, and like Cuba, it drew near the communist countries. Domínguez also concludes that, for Nicaragua as for Cuba, hostility to the United States was all but inherent. Ortega, like Castro, was from the start a radical, not a reformer. Thus, it is hard to imagine an alternative history of the revolution with regard either to its neighbors or to the United States.

Revolutions as Security Threats

The instance of Nicaragua, physically small and economically trivial, underscores the question of what accounts for the U.S. impulse to intervene against Latin American revolutions. All the authors emphasize ideology, and Kurth suggests that among the several reasons why the United States was able to accommodate the Cárdenas government in Mexico in the 1930s was that Cárdenas led a particularly indigenous revolution, one apart from foreign governments or ideologies. Not so Cuba or Nicaragua, for their Marxist-Leninist ideologies connected them directly to the Soviet Union and its allies.

Robert Pastor, noting that "national security" is subjective, relative, and changing, sets out a series of U.S. arguments for opposing revolutions. The

United States did not initially oppose revolution in Mexico, Cuba, or Nicaragua, and it has not always supported right-wing governments. Still, Pastor accepts the history of U.S. hostility to leftist revolutionaries.

He finds fault with several conventional interpretations of why. That Washington opposes revolution for the sake of world capitalism is belied by the small and declining U.S. economic stakes in the region. That Washington does so to sustain its hegemony or sphere of influence seems to deny that any real U.S. interests exist in the region. It also makes of the interest that all states share in the internal politics of their neighbors something qualitatively different for the United States.

If the hegemonic argument sees tangible U.S. interests in Latin America as weak, the national security perspective, for Pastor, makes the opposite error, seeing unlimited threats to be countered by limitless means. Pastor's final perspective accepts that revolutions can threaten U.S. interests but are likely to do so indirectly, in ways that affect the nations of the region at least as much as the United States. The U.S. response should be not limitless but proportional to the nature of the threat.

For Marcial Pérez Chiriboga, writing as a Venezuelan, national security cannot be defined too narrowly; it is not simply defense of national territory. It also includes a concern for what happens in the region, though for Venezuela the zone is smaller than for a great power like the United States. And his definition has an ideological content in its commitment to fostering democracy.

Do Marxist-Leninist revolutions threaten Latin American states? Perez Chiriboga's answer, not so different from Pastor's, is that they can, though do not inevitably. They can through training dissidents, shipping arms, or the like. Capacity also matters; thus a massive increase in military force by a revolutionary state is destabilizing, by threatening an arms race. At the same time, Perez Chiriboga makes plain that unilateral U.S. interventions against revolution are also dangerous to the interests of a conservative democracy like Venezuela.

The Experience of Contadora

All the authors make proposals for breaking the impasse, imagining new bargains, explicit or implicit, that might secure the interests of both the United States and Latin America. Domínguez, however, doubts the conditions for such a bargain are in place, for, as Kurth notes, both the United States and Latin America need to forswear their practices of the last decade—the United States by separating serious threats from minor ones; revolutionary regimes by exercising self-restraint; and Latin American states by being prepared to add a military dimension, if need be, to collective diplomacy. Muñoz recommends a combination of measures to withdraw the military presence of the superpowers from the region and to construct regional and subregional mechanisms within it.

Pastor echoes Kurth's call for the United States to discriminate. And he emphasizes that the United States has a stake in collective action. If a revolutionary regime does come to power, one legitimate objective can be realized by the United States alone—preventing the revolution from establishing a military relationship with the Soviet Union or Cuba. Two others, however, require cooperation with Latin American states—preventing arms shipment to other revolutionaries, and expanding the prospects for democracy in the revolutionary state.

Near the center of these suggestions, and running through all our conversations, was the yet unfinished peace process in Central America, first the Contadora process, then the Arias plan. Do they represent one part of the bargain—the taking of responsibility by Latin Americans—which ought to call forth the other, a forswearing of intervention by the United States? Carlos Rico's chapter explores that question through the early years of the Contadora process.

Surely it is striking that the four Contadora countries—Colombia, Panama, Mexico and Venezuela—came together at all, and more striking still that the Central Americans themselves later took control of the process, under the leadership of Costa Rica's President Oscar Arias. The groupings were a sharp break with Latin American history, which had been one of passivity even in the face of concerns over U.S. activity. The formation of the "Contadora support group," initially comprising Argentina, Brazil, Peru, and Uruguay, suggested the broader Latin American application of techniques developed to deal with Central America. Rico stresses, however, that it was the fear of U.S. action, a direct military intervention, that impelled the Latin American participants to act.

Still, whatever the hopes surrounding the early years of the process, it did not then succeed, and Rico assesses why. The willingness of the United States to reach a negotiated settlement that would leave the Sandinista regime in power was in doubt, to put it gently, and the involved Latin American countries were quite different in size, politics, and stakes in Central America. The Central Americans were condemned to share a strategic space with a superpower, the United States, while for the South Americans, Central America was less immediate and played a smaller role in both "their foreign policy agendas and in their domestic political debates."

The initial diagnoses of the United States and the Contadora counties were sharply different. Put in Kurth's terms, the United States saw the roots of the problem as external, the Contadora countries as internal. While the former thus sought to isolate Nicaragua, the latter wanted to insulate Central America from the broader East-West antagonism: the United States called for basic change in the Sandinista regime; the Contadora countries worked toward arrangements that would permit the Sandinistas to live in peace with their neighbors. In this light, the Arias initiative of 1986 reflected a move toward the U.S. definition of the problem—the internal nature of the Nicaraguan state was placed squarely on the agenda.

Reshaping Collective Security

Richard Bloomfield's conclusion bring the strands of recommendation together. He argues that the American interventionist impulse runs deep. For Bloomfield, it is deeply ideological: it is, after all, democracy, not race or religion or cultural history, that unites Americans. And the United States had never been isolationist with respect to the Western Hemisphere. Hence, hopes that intervention will fade with the sea change in U.S.-Soviet relations may be premature: witness the American invasion of Panama at the end of 1989.

If collective security in the Americas is to be reshaped, the United States will have to live down the burden of history, including that of the OAS. That implies that the United States should stay in the background, giving subregional groups space to try to resolve security issues. Only if they were not able to do so would wider groupings involving the United States come into play.

For Bloomfield, Contadora suggests that one condition for such a collective security arrangement is in place. All the Latin American nations involved had reason not to cross the United States, yet all felt they had powerful national interest in doing so. Will a comparable cost-benefit calculation for the United States indicate a comparable break with past practice? For most of the postwar period, the United States was willing to bear the cost of being perceived as *the* interventionist power in the hemisphere, but the costs may be higher now, reflected in the divisive internal debate over Nicaragua and the resulting inattention to other hemispheric problems like drugs and immigration.

A change for the United States will, however, require a change in mindset, in the ideologically driven national security doctrine discussed by several of the authors. Mikhail Gorbachev is making the change easier by seeming to take the Soviet Union out of the competition, at least for now. The United States will retain plenty of force to deal with real threats to its security, and it should make plain its willingness to do so. Nor need a more discriminating policy imply ceasing to care about democracy in the hemisphere, only that the United States stop short of overthrowing regimes to advance that interest.

And so the question returns to the Latin Americans: will they take more responsibility for dealing with security problems in the hemisphere so that the

United States can take less? For all its fits and starts, the results thus far of the Central American peace process are hopeful. Panama is less so, although the failure may be less stark than it seemed at first blush. General Noriega was not a security threat by the definition of this book—he did not threaten to invade or destabilize his neighbors. Thus, there was merit to the Latin American argument that he was less a security threat than a possible U.S. invasion. Neither the Reagan nor the Bush administration was really interested in cooperating with the Latin Americans, though the latter did make one belated attempt. In these circumstances, it is perhaps surprising that the Latin American states went as far as they did, voting in the OAS in 1989 to seat Noriega's opponents.

Still, the pattern was familiar. The United States looked, if belatedly, for clear support from the Latin Americans and did not get it. Latin Americans feared U.S. intervention and got it. There is still a chance to reshape collective security in the hemisphere, but it will have to be built on the ashes of Panama. Panama, which occurred after our deliberations, makes the task we undertook all the more pointed.

Note

1. C. Neale Ronning, *Intervention in Latin America* (New York: Knopf, 1970), p. 3.

1

The Rise and Decline of the Inter-American System: A U.S. View

James R. Kurth

The Inter-American System and the Atlantic Triangle

The concept of an inter-American security system has had a long, and a troubled, history. The inter-American system that was formally established with the Inter-American Treaty of Reciprocal Assistance at Rio de Janeiro in 1947 and the Organization of American States at Bogota in 1948 had antecedents that reached back through the Inter-American Conferences and the Good Neighbor Policy of the 1930s and 1940s, through earlier Inter-American Conferences and the Pan-American Union of the 1890s through 1920s, to the Monroe Doctrine of 1823, and even back to the original idea of a New World separate and distinct from the Old.[1]

The essential purpose of any inter-American security system has always been not so much inter-American as anti-European; it has been a system opposed to the expansion of European power into the Americas, especially to the expansion of the greatest land power on the European continent at any particular time (e.g., Russia or Austria in the 1820s, Imperial Germany in the first decade of this century, Nazi Germany in the 1930s and 1940s, and the Soviet Union since the 1940s). This is because the true international system in which the countries of the Americas have found themselves since their origins has never really been an inter-American system composed of two major parts, North America and Latin America; rather, it has been an Atlantic basin system composed of three major parts, Europe, North America, and Latin America, or as Charles de Gaulle once put it, of "Europe and its daughters." The three parts of this system form a sort of triangle bounding the Atlantic Ocean. Western Europe is closer in miles to the eastern seaboard of the United States than is most of South America. And the Southern Cone of South America is as close to Western Europe as it is to the United States.

This reality has been particularly relevant to North Americans. Since the late seventeenth century, every great European war has spread across the Atlantic to become a war fully engaging the North Americans, either on their own territories (from the wars of Louis XIV through the Napoleonic Wars) or within Europe itself (the two World Wars).

In these wars the geographic position of Latin America in the Atlantic triangle, especially the position of the countries of the Caribbean basin, has always posed a potential threat to the lines of communication between the United States and its allies in Europe and at times a threat to the territory of the United States itself. Thus the United States, soon after independence, determined upon a policy of excluding the expansion of any European great power into the Americas, e.g., into Latin America in a way that could threaten North America. From the perspective of the United States, the benefits, indeed the necessity, of an inter-American (and anti-European) security system have always been obvious.

Within this international system of the Atlantic triangle, however, the perspective of most Latin American countries has been rather different. There have been times, of course, when particular Latin American countries might be threatened by the expansion of a European power (e.g., some of the newly independent countries in the 1820s, Mexico and the Dominican Republic in the 1860s, several Caribbean states in the 1890s and later), and on such occasions the perspective of these countries could be similar to that of the United States. But for the most part, Latin American governments could see the European part of the triangle not so much as a danger but as an opportunity, as a salutary balance to the North American part.

By the end of the nineteenth century, the most obvious threat of a new colonial power came from the Americas themselves, i.e., from the United States. The same balance of power logic, or realpolitik, that led the United States to exclude a European power from the Americas could lead Latin American countries to include it, and, in a reversal of the dictum of the British foreign secretary, George Canning, in 1823, to "call in the Old World to redress the imbalance in the New." A logic that only considered international security within the tripolar framework would not lead Latin America to support an inter-American security system with the same anxiety, energy, and consistency as the United States. To bring about Latin American support, some other factors or dimensions would have to be added to the equation. There have been three such dimensions: (1) regional international security, i.e., security against threats from other Latin American states; (2) internal security; and (3) international economy.

Regional International Security

This dimension is within the normal definition of international or collective security. If Latin American governments faced threats from their Latin American neighbors, an inter-American collective security system could be constructed upon two bases, the European or extra-American threat and the regional or intra-American one. The Latin American governments would support the United States against threats from European great powers, while the United States would support the Latin American governments against threats from other Latin American small powers. This would be a collective security system in the strict sense of the term.

This bargain is fine as far as it goes. But in the twentieth century, at least, the occasions when one Latin American country has threatened another with a clear act of aggression have been rather few. (One prominent case was Nicaragua's aggressions against Costa Rica in the 1940s and 1950s.) In themselves, such threats have not provided an extensive and solid enough basis for an inter-American security system. Merely considering international security, then, would lead to an inherent fragility and instability in any inter-American security system. An inter-American system could only become stable if yet another dimension were added, i.e., if considerations of international politics were supplemented by considerations of internal politics or of international economics.

Internal Security

If Latin American governments faced internal threats while the United States faced an external one, a collective security system could be constructed upon these two bases, especially if the major parties could agree that the external threat was in fact the source of the internal one. Thus, the unity of an inter-American security system would rest upon the disunity within many of its Latin American members. And this in fact has been the pattern on many occasions during the Cold War, especially in the 1960s, the decade after the Cuban revolution.

International Economy

Finally, if Latin American governments were unable to perceive any security threat at all, be it extra-American, intra-American, or internal, they still might be persuaded to arrive at a common definition of the threat with the United States if the United States was prepared to provide an array of economic benefits, if the inter-American security system actually included an inter-American economic system. In practice, these economic benefits have varied greatly among Latin American countries, among interest groups, and from one era to another; they have taken the forms of access to U.S. markets, direct investment by U.S. corporations, loans from U.S. private banks, and aid from U.S. government agencies. The best known program of U.S. aid was the Alliance for Progress in the early 1960s. Whatever they have been, however, these economic benefits have generally served some Latin Americans more than, and sometimes at the expense of, others.

Thus, the United States could best achieve its objective of international security in the Americas by meeting the Latin American objectives of internal security and/or economic opportunities. This has been the basic pattern, the deep structure, of inter-American relations since the beginning of the twentieth century. But the form these relations have taken has varied according to the nature of the threat from the dominant European power, the nature of the political conflicts within the Latin American states, and the level of socioeconomic development within these states.

In the first half of the twentieth century, the inter-American security system was largely shaped by the threat of Germany, first that of Kaiser Wilhelm and then that of Adolf Hitler; in the second half, it has largely been shaped by the threat of the Soviet Union, first by itself and then through its ally, Cuba. We shall discuss each of these eras in turn.

Imperial Germany and the Unilateral Inter-American Security System

The first and the simplest of these European threats came from Imperial Germany. With its great industrial power and its growing navy, the Germany of Kaiser Wilhelm represented a direct threat to the British global order and an indirect threat to the U.S. order in the Americas. Given the nature of the military technology of the time, this threat could be projected against the United States if Germany were to acquire its own colonies or allies and its own naval bases within the New World, and particularly within the Caribbean.

Germany, however, had no special advantage over Britain or the United States in regard to the internal politics of Latin American states. Whatever the differences between Latin and North American ideas and interests (and more generally Anglo-American ones), the Germany of Kaiser Wilhelm did not offer a model that was any more attractive. Nor could Imperial Germany offer economic benefits that were dramatically more attractive than those offered by Britain and the United States. Thus, the Germans could only gain a beachhead in the Americas in the three traditional ways of great power diplomacy: (1) acquiring a colony and base directly from another European state (e.g., the Caribbean colonies of Spain or the Danish West Indies); (2) acquiring political control of an independent state indirectly through the administration of its finances (e.g., the Dominican Republic and Haiti); and (3) acquiring an ally by offering protection and support against threats from the United States (e.g., revolutionary Mexico).

The first of these threats was the most familiar; the Monroe Doctrine and the related No-Transfer Doctrine had addressed it directly eighty years before. It was also the easiest for the United States to confound; in the case of the Spanish and the Danish colonies, the United States solved the problem through annexation (Puerto Rico, the Danish West Indies) or prohibition (Cuba, with the Platt Amendment).

The second threat, that of political control, the U.S. addressed with the Roosevelt Corollary, that is, preemptive intervention by the United States within the internal political processes of the countries at issue.[2] This method of countering a European threat would of course reappear again and again, even to the present day.

The method of the Roosevelt Corollary, U.S. intervention in internal politics, could of course increase the likelihood of the third kind of threat, i.e., a Latin American regime seeking the help of a European power to protect it against that intervention. This was the danger presented by Mexico in the the first decade of this century. And it would also be the danger presented again by Mexico in the 1930s, Guatemala in the 1950s, Cuba in the 1960s, and Nicaragua in the 1980s. In the first case, however, it happened that for other reasons the United States immediately and directly transcended and resolved the threat by going to war with Imperial Germany and bringing about its defeat.

The brief period of the threat from Imperial Germany thus prefigures in certain ways the dynamics of later periods of threat from a dominant European power: (1) the socioeconomic development of Latin American states had reached the point that they were open to penetration by an expanding European power; (2) the United States sought to eliminate this threat by intervening directly in the political processes of some of these states; this in turn led to (3) a threatened state becoming susceptible to receiving the support of that European power. This pattern would reappear in each of the succeeding eras. However, in the first era, the actions of the United States were almost wholly unilateral and did not involve seeking the cooperation of other Latin American states; there was nothing collective about this inter-American security system. This approach would not reappear again until the 1980s.

Nazi Germany and the Multilateral Inter-American Security System

With the defeat of Imperial Germany in World War I, the European threat disappeared, if only temporarily. This, of course, did not prevent the United States from continuing to engage in unilateral interventions during the 1920s, particularly in Nicaragua, the Dominican Republic, and Haiti, but these interventions had little to do with U.S. security interests. They were undertaken for lesser objectives, i.e., to preserve U.S. political influence, maintain local political stability, or protect U.S. economic interests. It has often been the case with great powers (Britain and the Soviet Union provide other examples) that a series of foreign interventions begins for reasons of international security, but the practice of intervention then becomes so institutionalized that the later interventions are undertaken for lesser political or economic purposes.[3]

The Great Depression brought about an intensification of isolationism for the United States. The domestic support for U.S. military interventions to maintain political and economic interests abroad was greatly reduced, and the Hoover administration proceeded to reduce U.S. military involvement in the Caribbean and Central America, particularly in Nicaragua.

Given the rather benign international environment of the time and given the isolationist consensus within the United States, it was relatively easy in 1933 for the new administration of Franklin Roosevelt to adopt the Good Neighbor Policy, whereby the United States would refrain from intervention in the internal politics of Latin American states and would engage in close consultations with Latin American governments on security concerns. The Good Neighbor Policy of the second Roosevelt administration in large measure repealed the Corollary of the first.[4]

In the next few years, however, new and serious issues of international security arose, especially in Mexico and in Argentina.

The Mexican Problem

Mexico in the late 1930s posed a problem with potentially grave consequences. In 1938, the government of President Lázaro Cárdenas nationalized the properties of U.S. (and British) oil companies, raising the possibility of a classic conflict between the Mexican and the U.S. governments. The actual outcome, however, was very different and represents something of a model in inter-American relations.

On the one hand, President Franklin Roosevelt recognized that the vital interest of the United States was not the protection of particular U.S. companies, but the protection of U.S. national security against an expanding Nazi Germany. This required a friendly nation on the southern border of the United States and the reestablishment of mutual interests between the United States and Mexico, which meant acceptance of the nationalizations, a vital interest for Mexico at the time. Roosevelt understood that the United States had great strategic and economic strengths, that the Mexican leadership would in turn recognize this, and that a Mexico that was politically independent while nestled within a U.S. strategic and economic framework was a far surer friend than a resentful and hostile Mexico looking for a foreign protector, which at the time could have been Nazi Germany (as Imperial Germany had nearly become in World War I).

On the other hand, President Lázaro Cárdenas could also be understanding of the vital interest of the United States. Mexico had begun its revolution in 1910, before either the Marxist revolution in Russia in 1917 or the Fascist movements in Europe of the 1920s and 1930s. The Mexican revolution was an authentically *American* revolution. Although the national populism of the Mexican revolution did acquire certain ideas from the Russian revolution after 1917, it essentially remained free of the ideologies of European powers. Indeed, Cárdenas appears to have consciously modeled some of his policies after those of Roosevelt's New Deal. Thus, in the 1930s the United States and Mexico each had a leader who could understand the vital interests of the other and who made efforts to reassure the other that his government would not threaten those vital interests. The result was a sort of "historical compromise" between the two nations.

The Argentine Problem

National populism also posed a serious problem for the United States in the nations of the Southern Cone, especially in Argentina. Here, national populism took a more European form. The Argentine military coup of June 1943 brought into power a government that was highly nationalist and consequently was opposed to British and U.S. influence in Argentine affairs. The nationalist regime also soon acquired a populist character, with the urban labor movement led by Colonel Juan Perón. From a U.S. perspective, national populism in Argentina appeared to have obvious affinities with Fascism in Italy and with National Socialism in Germany. There seemed to be no possibility of pursuing a Mexican-style solution, given the European coloration of the Argentine regime.[5]

The Roosevelt administration therefore sought to alter and/or isolate the new Argentine government. This objective took on greater urgency with an Argentine-supported military coup in Bolivia in December 1943. Despite severe disagreement within the Department of State about the best course, the Roosevelt administration was for the most part consistent in following the principles of the Good Neighbor Policy. The administration also worked closely with other Latin American governments to arrive at a consensus solution for collective pressure upon the Argentine regime.

The Argentine problem largely became moot with the defeat of Nazi Germany in 1945. Although there would still be another year of mutual acrimony, both the Truman administration and the Perón regime came to recognize that there was no longer any irreconcilable conflict of interests between the United States and Argentina, and a period of mutual acquiescence ensued.

The brief period of threat from Nazi Germany also prefigures certain features of later periods of threat from the Soviet Union. (1) Again, the socioeconomic development of Latin American states had reached the point that they were open to penetration by an expanding European power, but by now the level of development in some states meant that there was for the first time a large popular sector, a potential mass base for that penetration. (2) This time, however, the United States sought to eliminate this threat not by direct intervention in a state's internal politics but by extended and responsive negotiations, either with the national populist regime itself (most significantly Mexico, but also Brazil under Vargas) or with other Latin American governments through inter-American conferences (as regarding Argentina). In this second period, the actions of the United States were often multilateral; the inter-American security system became a collective one. (3) As a result, the Latin American states became less, rather than more, susceptible to receiving the support of the European power.

The Soviet Union and the Institutionalization of the Inter-American Security System

The era of the Roosevelt administration, of the Good Neighbor Policy and World War II, established the fundamental principles and practices of the inter-American collective security system. They were institutionalized in the Inter-American Treaty of Reciprocal Assistance at Rio de Janeiro in 1947 and the Organization of American States at Bogota in 1948. The explicit principles of the system were two, nonintervention and collective security. Each principle met the vital interests of one of the two parties, the United States or Latin America, and implied responsibilities for the other. On the one hand, nonintervention meant that the United States would not intervene in the internal politics of Latin American states (a repeal of the corollary of the first Roosevelt). On the other hand, collective security meant that the Latin American states would join with the United States to exclude from the Americas the threat of a dominant European power (which was now the Soviet Union). The new inter-American collective security system thus was founded upon a reciprocal exchange, "a great bargain," between the United States and Latin America.

The meaning of the first principle, nonintervention, was quite clear. The meaning of the second, collective security, was more problematic. For one thing, who would define what was a threat to the Americas? Was a threat to the United States (which was obviously in the Americas) also a threat to the Americas (which was not so obvious)?

The Roosevelt administration's practices and the Good Neighbor Policy had filled in one possible meaning of the principle of collective security. The

United States expected the Latin American states largely to accept its definition of what was a threat to the Americas. This expectation was in the nature of a great power; it was certainly in the nature of a great power whose population (in 1945) of 140 million citizens equaled the population of all of Latin America, which had just fought its greatest foreign war against a dominant European power, and which had just assumed the responsibility for the security of virtually all of Western Europe. However, the U.S. would also consult with Latin American governments in extended discussions and in good faith to bring about a common understanding of the U.S. definition of the threat. And the United States would be open to accepting modifications of its definition, where peripheral rather than vital U.S. interests were at stake. This had been the practice of the United States in the issue of Argentina in 1943-1945.

On their part, the Latin American governments quite naturally hoped that this mutual understanding of inter-American security interests would come about with more mutual benefits from inter-American economic relations, that the United States government would undertake a vigorous and sustained program of economic aid to Latin America. The Good Neighbor Policy, especially during the boom years of World War II, seemed to have had attached to it something of an economic clause. The Latin American governments, therefore, were greatly disappointed at Bogota in 1948 when Secretary of State George Marshall did not offer a Marshall Plan for Latin America. Most U.S. administrations have recognized the existence of this implicit economic clause of the inter-American security system, and they have made some effort to abide by it. Thus, there was the Point Four Program of the Truman administration, the Alliance for Progress of the Kennedy administration, and U.S. government support of private bank lending from the Nixon administration through the Reagan administration. But the Latin American governments have continued to be disappointed even to the present day.

The new institutions of the inter-American collective security system were soon confronted with two serious tests. The first and most serious was in Guatemala. A second was in Bolivia.

The Guatemalan Revolution

The Guatemalan revolution began as a national populist movement. Like the national populist movements in Mexico, Argentina, and Brazil, it was shaped by the circumstances at the time of its birth, in this case, by the appeals of Marxism. In Guatemala, populism was based more upon an agricultural working class and less upon an urban middle class than it was elsewhere. Thus an archetypical pattern of danger for the United States soon arose: (1) a national-populist regime adopting the ideological and, in some measure, the institutional forms of the greatest European power (now the Soviet Union);

(2) the regime undertaking the expropriation of U.S. investments and the assertion of national identity against the United States; this gave rise to (3) the potential for U.S. intervention; in turn (4) this drove the regime to even closer relations with that European power.

What were the possible outcomes of the Guatemalan problem given the principles and practices of the inter-American collective security system? There were three possible models or paths that could be drawn from the past: (1) the Caribbean, i.e., unilateral U.S. interventions, like the U.S. had undertaken in various states in the Caribbean basin through the 1920s; (2) the Mexican, i.e., a bilateral settlement with the revolutionary government; and (3) the Argentine, i.e., multilateral negotiations through inter-American institutions to arrive at a consensus method of resolving the problem. It was the first path that the United States eventually chose, but the other two are worth some discussion.

The Mexican Model

This path would have followed the Mexican example, as we have described it in the previous section. On the one hand, the United States would have recognized the legitimacy of Guatemala's expropriation of the properties of U.S. companies (United Fruit and International Railways of Central America) and indeed might have worked closely with Guatemala to bring about acceptable compensation. This was the proposal of some career officials of the State Department during the Truman administration—those who were most loyal to the Good Neighbor Policy and felt an obligation to continue it.[6]

On the other hand, the Guatemalan government of Juan José Arévalo, and then Jacobo Arbenz, like that of the Mexican government of Cárdenas, would have recognized the legitimacy of the United States' exclusion of any Soviet penetration and would have reassured the United States to this effect. Specifically, the Guatemalan government would have given assurances that Guatemala would not acquire arms or advisors from the Soviet Union or its allies and that it would exclude local communists from positions of political power. This the Guatemalan government did not provide.

It is not surprising, then, that the new Eisenhower administration, which had no particular loyalty to the Good Neighbor Policy, determined to work toward the overthrow of the Arbenz regime. This still left, however, a choice between two paths, one multilateral and one unilateral.

The Argentine Model

One path would have followed the Argentine example, that is, turning to the inter-American collective security system in order to construct a truly collective or multilateral solution to the problem. On the one hand, the United

States would have engaged in extended consultations with the other Latin American states to arrive at a consensus as to how to deal with Guatemala. What that consensus would have looked like is difficult to say, but geographical proximity and political affinities would have had Mexico play a substantial role. Here, too, was a policy preferred by the career officials of the State Department, right down to the actual CIA-organized intervention in June 1954 (indeed, the plan for that intervention was kept secret from virtually all State Department officials until it occurred).[7]

On the other hand, the Latin American states would have recognized the legitimacy of excluding any Soviet penetration of a Latin American country and would have actively assisted the United States in achieving this. We do not really know if the Latin American states would have provided this, since the OAS track was short-circuited, "overtaken by events," by the CIA track, and an OAS meeting scheduled for July 1954 was never held.

The Guatemalan case represented a retreat by the United States from collective security and a return to unilateral security (although with a certain amount of collective legitimation by the OAS of the U.S. unilateral action). As such, the institutions of the inter-American collective security system did not pass their first serious test. It was not so much that they failed, but that they were never put to the test.

The Bolivian Revolution

The United States confronted a second revolutionary situation in Latin America about the same time that it confronted one in Guatemala. A revolution in Bolivia in April 1952 brought into power a national populist regime, one that included figures from the earlier Argentine-supported revolution of December 1943. In this case, however, the Truman administration and then the Eisenhower administration engaged in extensive negotiations with the revolutionary government, reached accommodation over a number of decisive issues (compensation for expropriation of U.S. investments, the role of radical labor leaders), and eventually provided substantial economic aid to the new regime. What explains the difference in outcomes between Bolivia and Guatemala?

First, the very roots of the Bolivian revolution in the earlier Argentine example meant that it would have less affinity with the Marxist model. In addition, the weight of U.S. investments in the Bolivian economy was much less than in the Guatemalan one, and this expropriation involved lesser stakes. Finally, and perhaps most significantly, the leadership of the Bolivian revolution, like Cárdenas earlier, made special efforts to be understanding of U.S. vital interests and concerns and to reassure U.S. officials of this in a variety of ways.

The Cuban Revolution and the North-Americanization
of the Inter-American Security System

The Cuban Revolution

Given the success of its Guatemalan enterprise, it is not surprising that the United States would use the same methods when the next major test of the inter-American security system arose, which was the Cuban revolution.

As in Guatemala, the United States attempted to overthrow the Castro regime in Cuba by means of CIA-organized intervention, most dramatically at the Bay of Pigs in April 1961 but also with economic sabotage and attempts to assassinate Castro. The U.S. also sought to isolate Cuba and to legitimate that isolation by organizing the OAS to suspend Cuba from membership and to back the United States fully in the Cuban Missile Crisis of 1962.[8]

In one sense, these efforts of the U.S. and the OAS ended in an obvious failure. The CIA interventions failed to overthrow the Castro regime, and in its direct negotiations with the Soviet Union during the missile crisis, the United States agreed not to invade Cuba in the future. As such, the inter-American security system failed to secure the fundamental objective of removing a regime allied to the Soviet Union.

In another sense, however, the Cuban case represented something of a success for the inter-American security system. For almost two decades after the Bay of Pigs and the Cuban Missile Crisis, the impact of the Cuban revolution and the Soviet expansion was largely limited to Cuba itself. In terms of inter-American security, the Cuban revolution by the mid-1960s was effectively contained within Cuba. Further, within the OAS, the Latin American countries had given the United States virtually everything that could reasonably be expected, given the different interests and perspectives that we have described.

The Dominican Crisis

This kind of success for the inter-American security system was even more pronounced in the next major test, namely, the Dominican crisis of 1965.

Just as the United States had (mistakenly) learned from the success of the CIA-organized intervention in Guatemala that such an intervention would work in Cuba, so it (probably mistakenly) learned from the failure of the CIA intervention in Cuba that a full military intervention would be necessary to prevent a communist regime, "a second Cuba," in the Dominican Republic. With that military intervention, one principle of the inter-American security system, that of nonintervention, was completely abandoned, and the corollary of the first Roosevelt was fully restored.

However, the other principle of the inter-American security system, that of collective security, remained firmly in place. The United States sought and received from the OAS collective legitimation of its intervention (by a bare two-thirds majority, composed of authoritarian regimes). It also sought and secured an Inter-American Peace Force, in which (largely token) military units from other Latin American states joined the U.S. military forces within the Dominican Republic, with the Peace Force as a whole formally under the command of a Brazilian general. The Dominican intervention represented the extreme point of an inter-American collective security system created in the image and defined by the interest of the United States.

The Cuban and Dominican episodes in the 1960s were thus the high point of the inter-American collective security system conforming itself to the conceptions of the United States. The explanation for this phase lies in the dimensions of the great bargain that we have previously discussed.

In the early 1960s, many Latin American governments feared internal threats, which were in part inspired by the Cuban revolution. To counter this, they sought and received military aid and advisors from the United States. They also sought and, for a time with the Alliance for Progress, received economic assistance from the United States. More than at any time before or since, the United States provided for the two elements of the bargain that were most important to the Latin American governments, and these governments in turn were more willing than at other times to provide the elements that were important to the United States.

Within a decade, however, the conjunction of circumstances that had brought about this kind of inter-American collective security system had disintegrated. Indeed, the circumstances had been largely replaced by their opposites.

The Nicaraguan Revolution and the Exhaustion of the Inter-American Security System

By the 1970s, each of the elements of the great bargain had disappeared. First, the very intensity of the fear of Marxist movements had brought into being some of the most repressive regimes that Latin America had ever known. Indeed, some of these reached such a degree of systematic and organized repression that political scientists invented for them a new term, "bureaucratic-authoritarian regimes." The sources of these bureaucratic-authoritarian regimes lay not only in the Cuban revolution but in the hyperinflation and in the need for massive capital formation that characterized the more developed Latin American countries, particularly those in the Southern Cone.[9] Whatever the causes, however, the bureaucratic-authoritarian regimes were deeply offensive to liberal democrats in the United States, particularly in the U.S. Congress. By the 1970s, Congress had greatly diminished, or completely extinguished, U.S. military aid and advisors to these regimes.

Second, the dimension of economic assistance underwent a radical transformation. The Nixon administration and its successors believed that the proper and most effective way to have economic resources flow to Latin America was not through the U.S. government or international organizations but through investments and loans from private enterprise, i.e., multinational corporations and international banks. In the 1970s and 1980s from these nongovernmental sources, Latin America received far more capital than it had received under previous governmental programs. In this sense, the economic clause of the inter-American security system was being fulfilled more than ever before; but in another sense, this meant the abolition of the economic clause of that system. The massive investments and loans came not as part of a great bargain or package composed of security, political, and diplomatic interests, as well as economic ones; it came in a vast river that flowed completely outside the institutional territory of the security system.

Thus, by the late 1970s, two of the essential elements of the inter-American collective security system had largely collapsed. On the eve of the Nicaraguan revolution, the system was a very different one from that which had existed a decade-and-a-half before.

The Nicaraguan Revolution

In 1978 and 1979, the United States faced a situation similar to that of Cuba in 1958 and 1959. As the Somoza regime disintegrated and the Sandinista movement increased in power, the United States sought possible alternatives to a new Marxist revolutionary regime. As in the Dominican crisis, the U.S. attempted to organize through the OAS an Inter-American peace force, which would interpose itself between the Somocistas and the Sandinistas in Nicaragua and which would provide the military protection for a moderate political solution. The OAS, however, declined to support the U.S. in this proposal. In part this was because the Sandinista movement clearly enjoyed widespread acceptance among the Nicaraguan population and did not clearly show that it was determined upon an authoritarian Marxist path. However, these features had also been present to a degree with the leftist rebels in the Dominican Republic in 1965, and they had not precluded the OAS from supporting the Peace Force then. But in 1979, the crucial elements of the great bargain, and the ties of cooperation and consultation that went with them, had largely disappeared.

The 1980s and the Fragmentation of the Inter-American Security System

In the 1980s, the United States and Latin America were confronted by a cascade of major crises and problems: (1) the polarization of relations between Nicaragua and the United States to the point of armed conflict; (2) the brutal guerrilla war in El Salvador; (3) the acquisition by Cuba of weapons systems with offensive capabilities (MiG-23 aircraft and Foxtrot submarines); (4) the war between Argentina and Britain over the Malvinas (Falkland) Islands; (5) the U.S. military interventions in Grenada and Panama; and (6) the massive burden of foreign debt upon Latin American economies.[10]

Any one of these issues ranks in magnitude with the major events in the previous history of the inter-American security system. This is not to say that the OAS had not continued to do good works; its Inter-American Commission on Human Rights, for example, had undertaken valuable investigations. It does mean, however, that the OAS since the mid-1970s has become something like the United Nations since the mid-1950s: an international organization whose technical and professional agencies are active and beneficial but whose security and economic functions have withered away.

Where, then, can the inter-American collective security system be found today? It can be found in three places, with a place for each of its major principles or elements as they have been recently and radically redefined.

The principle of nonintervention has become the practice of unilateral intervention. This could be found in the foreign policy of the Reagan administration, broadened somewhat to include the acquiescence of an adjacent state (Honduras) in the case of Nicaragua or the legitimation by a new (and non-Latin American) international organization (the Organization of Eastern Caribbean States) in the case of Grenada. Ironically, however, in the one case where Soviet power was most concretely extended into the Americas (e.g., Soviet offensive weapons provided to Cuba), the Reagan administration did nothing, and there was no security system, be it multilateral or unilateral, at all.

The principle of collective security has become the practice of collective nonintervention. This could be found in the diplomatic efforts of the Contadora group of Latin American states, which sought to resolve the U.S.-Nicaraguan conflict. The proposals and draft treaties of the Contadora countries were characterized by the true spirit and principles of an inter-American collective security system. In many ways and at many times, these proposals represented the vital and enduring interests of Nicaragua and the United States better than did the Sandinista leadership or the Reagan administration themselves. But security must have for its ultimate support some military forces, if only to provide effective monitors along violent frontiers. And this the Contadora countries would not provide.

Finally, the economic element of the inter-American collective security system, the main effort of which has been to dissolve the debt burden and to resolve the debt crisis, is to be found in two international organizations that are very different from the OAS, i.e., the International Monetary Fund and the World Bank.

Can the inter-American collective security system be put back together again? To do so would probably require each of the parties to move beyond their practices of the last decade, and perhaps to move back to their practices of an earlier time.

For the United States, this would mean a willingness to undertake intervention only against a clear and present danger (e.g., Soviet offensive weapons in the Americas) or only as a last resort (i.e., after extended negotiations in good faith with a Latin American revolutionary regime and consultations with other OAS members); it would mean a return to the policy of Franklin Roosevelt. For a revolutionary Latin American regime, such as that in Sandinista Nicaragua, this would mean a willingness to explicitly and consistently reassure the United States that it would provide no access for Soviet-bloc military arms or advisors; it would mean a return to the policy of Lázaro Cárdenas. And for other Latin American states, it would mean a willingness to add to the collective diplomacy of the Contadora group the military support necessary for its effectiveness, to create and make available some sort of international peace force; this would mean a return to the practice or the means of the Inter-American Peace Force in the Dominican intervention, but serving the spirit or the ends of the Contadora process. And here the greatest of the Latin American states, Brazil and Mexico, have major capabilities and therefore could assume major responsibilities.

The inter-American collective security system has never been based upon an identity of interests between the United States and Latin America. It has always been based upon a great bargain in which the very different vital interests of each were served, usually at the cost of the peripheral interests of the other. But great bargains can only be struck and maintained if each party understands, about itself and about each of the other parties, which interests are vital and which are peripheral. A renewed inter-American collective security system will not be based upon a common view of the Old World from the standpoint of the New. It can, however, be based upon a common understanding and acceptance of just how different from each other we in the Americas really are.

Notes

1. On the history of the inter-American idea and of inter-American relations, see the following: Gordon Connell-Smith, *The United States and Latin America: An Historical Analysis of Inter-American Relations* (New York: John Wiley & Sons, 1974), and his earlier *The Inter-American System* (London: Oxford University Press, 1960); Arthur P. Whitaker, *The Western Hemisphere Idea: Its Rise and Decline* (Ithaca: Cornell University Press, 1965); and Federico G. Gil, *Latin American-United States Relations* (New York: Harcourt Brace Jovanovich, 1971).

2. Walter LaFeber gives an interesting interpretation of the transformation of the Monroe Doctrine by the Roosevelt Corollary in his "The Evolution of the Monroe Doctrine From Monroe to Reagan," (Durham, New Hampshire: University of New Hampshire, Center for International Perspectives, September 20, 1985). His more detailed analysis of the history of U.S. policy toward Central America is given in *Inevitable Revolutions: The United States in Central America* (New York: W.W. Norton, 1983).

3. James R. Kurth, "Economic Change and State Development," in *Dominant Powers and Subordinate States: The United States in Latin America and the Soviet Union in Eastern Europe,* ed. Jan F. Triska (Durham, North Carolina: Duke University Press, 1986), pp. 85-101.

4. Bryce Wood, *The Making of the Good Neighbor Policy* (New York: Columbia University Press, 1961).

5. Bryce Wood, *The Dismantling of the Good Neighbor Policy* (Austin: University of Texas Press, 1985), Chapters 2-6.

6. Wood, *The Dismantling of the Good Neighbor Policy,* Chapter 9; Cole Blasier, *The Hovering Giant: U.S. Responses to Revolutionary Change in Latin America* (Pittsburgh: University of Pittsburgh Press, 1976), Chapters 1-3, 6.

7. Wood, *The Dismantling of the Good Neighbor Policy,* pp. 174-185.

8. Blasier, *The Hovering Giant,* Chapter 6; Connell-Smith, *The United States and Latin America,* Chapter 7. A comprehensive and perceptive analysis of U.S.-Latin American relations from the 1960s to the 1980s is given in Abraham F. Lowenthal, *Partners in Conflict: The United States and Latin America* (Baltimore: Johns Hopkins University Press, 1987). On the Soviet presence in Latin America in the same period, see Cole Blasier, *The Giant's Rival: The USSR and Latin America* (Pittsburgh: University of Pittsburgh Press, 1983) and Robert S. Leiken, *Soviet Strategy in Latin America* (Washington, D.C.: Georgetown Center for Strategic and International Studies, 1983).

9. David Collier, ed., *The New Authoritarianism in Latin America* (Princeton, New Jersey: Princeton University Press, 1979).

10. Lowenthal, *Partners in Conflict,* provides an excellent review of the crises and problems confronting Latin America in the 1980s. Also see Kevin J. Middlebrook and Carlos Rico F., eds., *The United States and Latin America in the 1980s: Contending Perspectives on a Decade of Crisis* (Pittsburgh: University of Pittsburgh Press, 1986). I have discussed some of these issues in an essay in the latter volume, "The United States, Latin America and the World: The Changing International Context of U.S.-Latin American Relations," pp. 61-86.

2

The Rise and Decline of the Inter-American System: A Latin American View

Heraldo Muñoz

The inter-American security system is in a state of crisis. This diagnosis is now widely shared in view of the insignificant role, if any, that the system played in addressing the major security problems that have threatened the hemisphere in recent years, such as the Malvinas/Falklands war between Great Britain and Argentina; the Central American conflicts; the U.S. invasion of Grenada; the border disputes between Chile and Argentina or Ecuador and Peru; and, more recently, the Latin American foreign debt crisis. However, the present breakdown of the inter-American security system has a long history; at least throughout the last two decades, the concept and the institutions of hemispheric security have declined in prestige, credibility, and effectiveness.

This chapter will seek to identify the main causes of the collapse of the system—for at least its principal organizational structures—rather than attempt a detailed description of its ascent and consequent decay. In the last analysis, the explanations of the failure of hemispheric security are simple: first, the system was based on false assumptions such as the "Western Hemisphere idea" and the supposed equality between the member states; second, the United States and Latin America had highly divergent expectations with regard to the alliance, which later evolved into disenchantment and bitterness when the original hopes of one side (Latin America) were not fulfilled; and, third, the changes that took place internationally during the 1960s and 1970s became an additional disintegrating factor for the system. These three sets of factors converge on one central contradiction: the system provided security for the United States, but produced insecurity for Latin America.

The Original Flaws of the System:
False Assumptions and Divergent Expectations

Following World War II, the United States emerged as the undisputed world hegemonic power and built a complex network of collective security agreements, norms, and practices to ensure its position of dominance; this security network was seen as vital, particularly in consideration of the growing Soviet challenge.

The strategic-political relationship between the United States and Latin America was marked by the creation of the Rio Treaty of Reciprocal Assistance of 1947; the approval of the Charter of the Organization of American States (OAS) in 1948; and the now forgotten Pact of Bogota of 1948, which was to be an effective framework for the peaceful settlement of disputes in the hemisphere. Additionally, Washington promoted the creation of a veritable inter-American military system, as John Child has labeled it, through the implementation of security assistance programs, joint military maneuvers, and the creation of several military institutions of a hemispheric scope.[1]

The concept of "collective security" was incorporated specifically as a key component of the emerging inter-American system. Through the Rio Treaty it was understood that the United States would come to the defense of the hemisphere in the event of an extra-continental attack, while the OAS and the Bogota Pact were meant to be the essential mechanisms for mediation and peaceful settlement of regional conflicts.

The inter-American system was based upon two central principles that soon proved to be simply "myths": first, the "Western Hemisphere idea" and, second, the supposed equality between the member states of the system.[2]

The "Western Hemisphere idea" stemmed from the assumption that between the United States and Latin America there were "common interests." But, in reality, since the Monroe Doctrine was proclaimed in 1823, Washington has considered Latin America and the Caribbean largely as its exclusive area of influence. On the other hand, many countries of Latin America hoped that a "special relationship" would develop between the region and the United States, based upon a Pan-Americanist spirit; but, by the end of the 1940s, a wide spectrum of Latin American nations already perceived the United States as "a menace in her own right,"[3] and reasoned that perhaps an elaborate inter-American security structure could serve to limit Washington's interventionism in the hemisphere. Clearly, Latin America became aligned with Washington as the Cold War deepened. However, at the time, the real threat to the sovereignty of Latin American countries was posed by their northern neighbor rather than an extracontinental power.

The second myth underlying the inter-American system was the supposed equality between the member states of the system, recognized in all its treaties and founding declarations. But, in practice, the obvious asymmetry in the power relations between the United States and the region quickly emerged as a central feature of the system. In fact, it was understood in Washington that the security of the United States depended, to a significant extent, on the exercise of a firm hegemony over the region, and that independent behavior on the part of Latin American states, particularly if accompanied by growing ties with the Eastern bloc countries, implied a threat to such hegemony that had to be impeded or counteracted unilaterally, if need be.

The inter-American system also failed because the Latin American nations had very different expectations about the emerging hemispheric structure from those of the United States. As Van Klaveren has suggested, Latin America trusted that the system would involve: (1) an economic cooperation scheme similar to the Marshall Plan, and (2) a U.S. commitment to nonintervention as the basis for a harmonious inter-American relationship.[4] It soon became clear that Latin America was to be disappointed on both counts.

By the 1950s it was evident that Washington was reluctant to include economic issues in the inter-American agenda and, even more so, to elevate Latin America to equal partnership. This reluctance came despite the rhetoric of the "common interests" of the Western Hemisphere and despite Latin America's collaboration in the war effort[5] as well as in the construction of the post war international order.

From the very beginning the United States used the inter-American system to produce resolutions in line with its strategic objectives, ranging from a global condemnation of international communism to a declaration in favor of U.S. participation in the Korean War. But, when the hemispheric security machinery was too cumbersome to confront what Washington defined as challenges to its interests, it simply acted unilaterally. In Guatemala in 1954, the United States intervened first and went to the OAS later; in the regional organization it merely obtained a seal of approval for a policy that had already been decided. The same logic of unilateral actions was behind the Bay of Pigs invasion of 1961. Similarly, the invasion of the Dominican Republic in 1965 was also accompanied by a supportive resolution of the OAS and, most significantly, by the creation of an inter-American Peace Force for the occasion, despite the strong opposition of key Latin American countries, such as Chile, Mexico, Peru, and Uruguay. Thus, as Jerome Slater states, the United States legitimized its unilateral policies, but at the cost of delegitimizing the OAS and the collective security concept.[6]

By the mid-1960s, it was evident that the inter-American system was deteriorating rapidly as Latin American hopes vanished. The change in the international context from Cold War to détente surfaced as an additional factor in the process of decay of the system.

A New International Context
and New Problems for the System

In a more relaxed atmosphere characterized by the emergence of new regional powers, the recovery of Western Europe and Japan, the progressive decline of the old political-ideological blocs, and an improvement in relations between the United States and the USSR, and the United States and China, the Latin American nations tried to maximize the scope for autonomous foreign policy behavior and sought to defend their own economic interests, often in conflict with the United States. During this period a number of U.S. firms in Latin America were nationalized as various states, large and small, attempted to exercise full control over their national resources; at the same time, the countries of the region tried new integration schemes, such as the Andean Pact created in 1969.

One of the most significant signs of the change that was taking place in U.S.-Latin American relations was the formal delivery, by Chilean Foreign Minister Gabriel Valdes, of the "Viña del Mar Consensus," forged within the framework of CECLA (the Special Commission for Latin American Coordination), to President Richard Nixon in June 1969. The document stated that there existed "a profound crisis in the facts and in the institutions of the inter-American system"; that the interests of Latin America were not identical to those of Washington (on the contrary, the document asserted, these tended to be "progressively contradictory"); and that Latin America gave more than it received from the United States. The "Viña Consensus" provoked irritation in the White House and led to a cooling of relations between Washington and the leading countries of this Latin American initiative.[7]

With the arrival of the 1970s, new tensions developed between the United States and Latin America. Washington was still deeply involved in the Vietnam War and, thus, Latin America and the inter-American system were not foreign policy priorities. In turn, the region's dissatisfaction with the inter-American system and economic relations with the United States led to concrete reforms of the OAS. At the San Jose meeting of 1975, the Latin American nations introduced the notion of collective economic security for development as part of the hemispheric discourse on strategic matters, while the United States firmly opposed this expansion of the security concept. At the same 1975 conference, the Rio Treaty was modified to allow, among other points, the lifting of treaty sanctions by simple majority instead of the traditional two-thirds vote, thus facilitating rapprochement with Cuba. That same year the SELA (Economic System of Latin America) was formed as a regional coordination organization for economic issues, including Cuba and excluding the United States.

In the decade of the 1970s, U.S. military aid to the region declined sharply, largely due to the growth of opposition in the U.S. Congress to arms sales to the less developed countries. Consequently, Latin American nations, particularly those ruled by military regimes, engaged new arms suppliers in Europe and elsewhere and developed local armament industries. In this period, as well, several Latin American countries began to articulate their own geopolitical perspectives beyond the National Security Doctrine. Moreover, several institutions of the inter-American military system were either eliminated or severely criticized by Latin Americans.[8] Under the Carter presidency, which emphasized the promotion of human rights in Latin America, relations between Washington and the many military regimes deteriorated even further. By the late 1970s the United States did not control the region as it did during the late 1940s, when the Rio Treaty and the OAS were established.

In sharp contrast to the 1965 Dominican case, in June 1979 the foreign ministers of the OAS declined a U.S. proposal to set up a mission to negotiate a transition in Nicaragua and rejected the idea of sending a multilateral "peacekeeping force" to restore order in Managua. Instead, the OAS favored a motion of the Andean group that stimulated the Sandinista victory over the Somoza dictatorship. Not surprisingly then, when the Reagan administration decided to invade Grenada in 1983, the White House sought legitimacy and an "image of collective action" in the OECS (Organization of Eastern Caribbean States) and not in the OAS. Yet, the matter was addressed by the OAS, where an ample majority condemned the intervention and recommended the withdrawal of U.S. troops from the island.[9]

Even more so than in Grenada, the prevailing collective security doctrine and the inter-American security system suffered a fatal blow during the Malvinas/Falklands War involving Argentina and Great Britain. Although the war did not actually dismantle the system—nor did it signify a lasting breakdown of U.S.-Latin American relations—it did demonstrate the total ineffectiveness of the system as a collective security instrument. As Connell-Smith has observed, the OAS was unable to resolve a major conflict in the subcontinent, nor did it truly stand behind one of its members that was at war with an extracontinental power.[10] The war inflicted severe damage on the Rio Treaty, reinforcing the belief among the Latin American states that their security definitely could not be left in the hands of Washington and that, therefore, military self-reliance was essential.

Lastly, the inter-American security system has been absolutely ignored in the Central American conflict, despite the gross violation of Articles 18, 19, and 20 of the OAS Charter—which prohibit all forms of intervention by any member state(s) against another government of the organization—as is the case in the Reagan administration's "unofficial" war against Nicaragua. Unlike the past, however, Latin American countries have sought to fill the void left by the inaction of the inter-American system through the flexible mechanism of the Contadora group, whose purpose is to counter Washington's military approach to the crisis with concrete proposals for a peaceful, negotiated solution.

Beyond Contadora, the joint declaration of May 1983 by the presidents of Mexico and Brazil opposing U.S. intervention in Central America was illustrative of general Latin American sentiment against the resurrection of "big stick" practices by the Reagan administration. In this vein, a special meeting of SELA unanimously approved a resolution condemning the U.S. economic boycott of Nicaragua imposed in May 1985. In any case, the United States, on the one side for its own reason, and Latin America, on the other side for its own particular reasons as well, have arrived at the conclusion that the inter-American system must be disregarded when it comes to important matters like the Central American crisis or the external debt of the region.

The Essential Contradiction of the System: Security for the United States, Insecurity for Latin America

In the preceding pages we have identified the principal factors that explain the progressive fragmentation and decay of the inter-American security system. In the final analysis, these factors converge into one fundamental and lasting tension: the system has served the security interests of the United States while disregarding those of Latin America.[11]

The nations of Latin America also have specific security interests to defend (i.e., reducing U.S. and European protectionism, expanding access to new technologies and markets, managing the foreign debt problem), but these have been traditionally postponed or overlooked by the United States. Moreover, the defense of U.S. interests within the inter-American framework has been conducted on Latin American and Caribbean soil, often resulting in armed confrontation, the deaths of civilians, economic disarray, and an arms race among the countries of the region.

Security from a Latin American perspective surely involves, on a fundamental level, the classic elements of continuity of the nation and integrity of the territory. But, as we have already suggested, security in the region also signifies political security: that is, effective self-determination and nonintervention in the domestic affairs of the countries of the area. Therefore, Latin America's security in this aspect would require that the United States: first, abstain from intervening in the internal matters of Latin American nations and, second, initiate a process of dismantling the structures and logic of intervention that Washington built over the years in line with the doctrine of national security and counterinsurgency criteria.

Security in Latin America also incorporates a vital socioeconomic dimension: the internal capacity to solve critical social, economic, and political problems in an egalitarian and democratic fashion. These domestic issues cannot be confused with external security matters. However, Washington has traditionally viewed radical social change, especially when carried out by socialist-oriented leaders, as a potential threat to its external security interests. Ironically, then, the kind of U.S. attitude and behavior that tends to equate deep-seated social transformations with an external (Soviet) menace ultimately constitutes a threat to Latin American interests; specifically, it represents an obstacle to progressive socioeconomic and political change.

This does not mean to imply that the United States has systematically opposed social change in the region. On the contrary, the U.S. government has sometimes earnestly promoted socioeconomic reforms in Latin America. But, the United States' concern for the social and economic development of the region has been sporadic and has generally appeared when a security crisis required the solidarity of Latin America with Washington. This was the case with the Alliance for Progress in the aftermath of the Cuban revolution. This has also been the case with President Reagan's Caribbean Basin Initiative announced in 1982 and the proposals of the Kissinger Commission for Central America submitted in early 1984. In effect, these projects of the Republican administration were largely stimulated by a need to complement a military policy with an offer of economic cooperation that would make the former more acceptable. The direct linkage with defense criteria is the principal fault of these U.S. initiatives: when the original geopolitical threat dissipates, so do the development programs. Moreover, when such reform programs are accompanied by an effort on the part of Washington to overthrow some government by force, they are even less effective and more transitory in nature.

In Washington's eyes, the high value placed on the status quo often tends to be equated with political stability and only the basic aspects of democracy. This is why popular movements in favor of change towards full democratization are sometimes mistrusted by the United States. From a Latin American standpoint, though, the mere installation of the institutions of liberal democracy in the region, although extremely important, will not guarantee a democratic order unless political-institutional democracy is accompanied by profound socioeconomic transformations to sustain it. There is some hope in this regard though, as can be concluded from the wide consensus that emerged in the Inter-American Dialogue in favor of the proposition that socioeconomic changes in Latin America and the Caribbean do not necessarily constitute an automatic threat to U.S. national security.[12]

In sum, the United States has consistently emphasized the military and strategic dimensions of the inter-American security system; conversely, the Latin American countries, although not denying the military aspects of the relationship, have stressed economic and social issues, struggling for better terms in commercial, financial, and investment ties. The U.S. posture has always prevailed, either because of the Latin American inability to respond with a common, unified position, or because in moments of crisis Washington's demand for hemispheric solidarity has been accompanied by a temporary concern with the economic and social problems of the region, a preoccupation that ceases as soon as the narrow security goal has been achieved.

The continuing lack of communication between the United States and Latin America regarding hemispheric security is best demonstrated in the foreign debt debate. For the Reagan administration the external debt of Latin America could be solved, in essence, by stimulating private foreign investment and increasing exports.[13] For Latin American countries, by contrast, the debt problem is the major security threat that the region now faces and, subsequently, they have urged the creditor countries to participate in the effort to find a common answer to a problem that cannot be solved in purely economic terms. Suggestively, the Latin American nations have preferred to keep the debt burden issue out of the inter-American system and have created, instead, ad hoc mechanisms for its treatment, such as the Group of Cartagena.

Some Conclusions and Suggestions About Collective Security

The inter-American system has failed as a hemispheric security arrangement. Today, Latin American countries believe there are better ways to foster their security than to adhere to a rigid hemispheric alliance like the one established in the late 1940s through the Rio Treaty. This does not mean, however, that the whole inter-American system is useless. For example, the OAS—the main institution of the system—has played a positive role in recent years in the protection of human rights in Latin America through its ad hoc commission, and, occasionally, it has contributed to the settlement of disputes among its members.[14] Moreover, there is a need for a permanent linkage between Latin America and the United States, which could be well served by an adapted inter-American system, redesigned as a forum for hemispheric exchanges rather than as a continental military alliance.

Still, some kind of regional security arrangement is required to address the various types of conflicts that will almost inevitably occur in Latin America due to traditional rivalries, power disputes, or other variables. It has become increasingly accepted in Latin America that an alternative security scheme must involve a political agreement among the world powers to solidly support an effort of regional cooperation to prevent conflicts, coupled with a process of demilitarization and disarmament within Latin American and Caribbean countries. Such an alternative security arrangement must also involve a firm resolve on the part of Latin American and Caribbean countries to take collective action against those states within the region that commit acts of aggression or subversion against another.

The principal purpose of such an alternative security system—that has come to be known as the "Zone of Peace" option[15]—would be to separate Latin America and the Caribbean from the East-West conflict logic and to focus national energies on the process of domestic development. This raises the issue of "security for whom," putting the accent on the security of the popular sectors or the majorities of our nations. By the same token, it means that the security problems of the region are more economic, social, and political than military or strategic. In any case, the preferred security scheme would have to take into account not only the security interests of Latin America and the Caribbean, but also the national security interests and threat perceptions of the United States. Hence, the Zone of Peace proposal should involve:[16]

1. The withdrawal of all military bases and troops external to the region. This would obviously be a gradual process, but it would have to include the U.S. military presence in Panama, Honduras, and other countries; the Soviet deployment in Cuba; and the British presence in the Malvinas/Falklands.
2. The effective denuclearization of the region through the actual implementation of the Tlatelolco Treaty.
3. A plan to control arms spending and advance towards disarmament in the region, in line with the plan outlined by Peruvian President Alan García[17] or other similar proposals. A good beginning would be an agreement not to introduce sophisticated new weaponry into the area.
4. An effective regional mechanism to implement collective measures to counter acts of aggression or subversion by a Latin American or Caribbean state against another.
5. The full acceptance of this new regional statute on the part of the big powers.

The implementation of such an ambitious proposal would demand bilateral and subregional negotiations such as those that were carried out by the Contadora group. It would be unrealistic to attempt region-wide negotiations, particularly considering the Central American conflict; therefore, South America could be the immediate focus of a Latin American Zone of Peace.

A basic step in this direction of arms control and peace would be the implementation of "mutual confidence building measures." This concept, linked to the Helsinki agreement of 1975, refers to those actions that can "reduce the risks of armed conflict, misunderstandings, or miscalculations about military activities that could lead to suspicion or fear, particularly in situations where the states involved lack adequate information."[18] The Contadora group had proposed various ideas in this regard: thirty days prior notice of military maneuvers within a radius of thirty kilometers from the borders; invitation to observers from neighboring countries; prohibition of international military operations in the territories involved; elimination of arms transfers for irregular forces; reduction of foreign military advisors in the participating nations; mixed security commissions; and a regional system of communications to link the governments of the area.

All of this is easier said than done. A Zone of Peace in Latin America is, to say the least, a difficult task to accomplish since it would require a sustained commitment on the part of the countries directly involved as well as the cooperation of the superpowers. On the other hand, there is no other clear option in sight. The creation of such an alternative security scheme may be, in the end, illusory. However, the continuation of the inter-American collective security system would be even more unrealistic, since it has already proven to be ineffective.

Notes

1. See Jack Child, *Unequal Alliance: The Inter-American Military System, 1938-1978* (Boulder: Westview Press, 1980). For a critique of this book, see Heraldo Muñoz, "Beyond the Malvinas Crisis: Perspectives on Inter-American Relations," *Latin American Research Review*, no. 1 (1984): 158-172.

2. See Alberto Van Klaveren, "The United States and the Inter-American Political System" in *Latin American Views of U.S. Policy*, ed. Heraldo Muñoz and Robert Wesson (New York: Praeger, 1986).

3. Jack Child, quoted by Gabriel Marcella, "The U.S.-Latin American Strategic Relationship: East-West or North-South" (Paper presented at the conference, "Securidad Nacional y Paz en America Latina," Instituto de Estudios Internacionales, Universidad de Chile, Viña del Mar, November 1984), p. 8.

4. A. Van Klaveren, "Inter-American Political System," pp. 22-24.

5. For instance, the estimates of Chile's contribution to the war due to the arbitrary price ceiling imposed on copper by the allies range from US$107 million to US$500 million. See Theodore Moran, *Multinational Corporations and the Politics of Dependence: Copper in Chile* (Princeton, New Jersey: Princeton University Press, 1977), p. 61.

6. See Jerome Slater, "The Limits of Legitimization in International Organizations: The OAS" in *Contemporary Inter-American Relations*, ed. Yale Ferguson (Englewood Cliffs, New Jersey: Prentice-Hall, 1972), pp. 204-226.

7. On this subject see Heraldo Muñoz and Carlos Portales, *Amistad Esquiva: Las Relaciones de Estados Unidos y Chile* (Santiago: Pehuen, 1987). This book is also forthcoming in an updated English edition as *Elusive Friendship: A Survey of U.S.-Chilean Relations* (Boulder: Lynne Rienner).

8. See Child, *Unequal Alliance*, pp. 197-236.

9. The Grenada invasion was indeed favored by the Caribbean countries that collaborated with it, but it deepened the differences within CARICOM and those between the Caribbean and Latin America. See U.S. Congress, House Committee on Foreign Affairs, *The English-Speaking Caribbean: Current Conditions and Implications for U.S. Policy*, 99th Cong., September 1985.

10. Gorden Connell-Smith, "The OAS and the Falklands Conflict," *The World Today* 38, no. 9 (September 1982): 340-347.

11. On this subject my views are based on the discussion at the conference, "Las Relaciones America Latina-Estados Unidos en la Segunda Mitad de los 80," organized by the Instituto de Estudios de Estados Unidos, CIDE, Mexico City, September 1984, in which this author and several other Latin American colleagues participated.

12. The Inter-American Dialogue, which gathered distinguished private citizens from the United States and Latin America and the Caribbean, states in its first document that it is convenient to keep the East-West conflict out of the region, and that this purpose is not served if "the United States opposes changes in the region simply because they diminish U.S. influence and hence are perceived as advantageous to Cuba and the Soviet Union, unless they are clearly related to basic security concerns" See Inter-American Dialogue, *The America at a Crossroads* (Washington, D.C.: Woodrow Wilson Center, April 1983), p. 42.

13. The Baker Plan announced by the United States in October 1985 at the joint meeting of the IMF and World Bank in Seoul represented a slight change towards a political solution of the debt problem of Third World nations. In Latin America, however, the Baker Plan was viewed as highly insufficient.

14. The classic example is the successful mediation of the OAS in the Honduras-El Salvador war of 1969. However, evidence shows that "virtually all of the successful mediation efforts of the inter-American system succeeded because of ad hoc arrangements utilized by forceful personalities." See Ronald Scheman and John W. Ford, "The Organization of American States as Mediator" in *International Mediation in Theory and Practice*, ed. S. Touval and I.W. Zartman (Boulder: Westview Press, 1985), pp. 197-231.

15. The idea of establishing Zones of Peace in various regions of the world was first introduced and approved in a Special Session of the United Nations in June 1978.

16. See Carlos Portales, "Zona de Paz: Una Alternativa a los Desafios Estrategicos de America Latina" (FLACSO, Santiago, November 1984, Mimeographed), pp. 23-24.

17. The text of the disarmament proposal of Alan García is reproduced in Hugo Palma, *America Latina: Limitacion de Armamentos y Desarme en la Region* (Lima: CEPEI, 1986), pp. 202-204.

18. Jozef Goldblat quoted by Gabriel Millan, "Mecanismos para Aumentar la Confianza Mutua en America Latina" (Paper presented at the conference "Seguridad Regional y Paz en America Latina," IEI, Universidad de Chile, Viña del Mar, November 12-22, 1984), p. 1.

3

The United States, Revolutionary Regimes in Cuba and Nicaragua, and Inter-American Collective Security

Jorge I. Domínguez

The United States in the twentieth century has found it difficult to coexist with revolutionary regimes in Latin America and the Caribbean. For many, of course, that is an appropriate stance: they have never seen a revolution that they liked, and they believe that it should be U.S. policy to prevent the consolidation, and promote the overthrow, of revolutionary regimes. For others, despite differences in particular cases, this has been a misguided policy for one or more of the following reasons: because it fails to distinguish among the values served by each revolution; because it accords greater weight than warranted to revolutionary regimes as a threat to the security of the United States and its allies; or because it perceives the job such regimes do, on balance, as desirable.

Two themes emerge from this array of views: values and interests. The various positions begin with a perspective on what a "good and acceptable" regime might be for the United States, and go on to make judgments about its impact on U.S. interests. Therefore, we will examine the values and the interests that have informed U.S. approaches to Latin America, and especially to the Cuban and Nicaraguan revolutionary regimes, relating the latter to inter-American collective security.

Values and Interests

"We owe it therefore to candor," President James Monroe said in his message of December 2, 1823, addressing the major European powers, "to declare that we should consider any attempt on their part to extend their system to any portions of this Hemisphere, as dangerous to our peace and safety." This unilateral statement, without even the force of U.S. law, has informed and summarized U.S. thinking toward its southern neighbors ever since. Presidents have changed but the perspective has endured; when it has seemed to weaken, the opposition has reminded the incumbent of Monroe's perpetual relevance.

The so-called "Monroe Doctrine" is most often interpreted as a strategic or geopolitical statement about U.S. interests. Indeed it is, but it is also an ideological statement. Monroe referred not to their influence, troubling as that was, but to "their system." His text makes it clear that the president was discussing ideological matters, too. The "political system" of the European powers, he asserted, "is essentially different . . . from that of America." It was the joint effect of interests and values that alerted Monroe to the threat beyond the oceans and that combination has triggered vigorous U.S. responses ever since.[1]

The self-image of the United States is pragmatic and nonideological, but that has rarely been the case in U.S. policy toward Latin America. At issue is a set of beliefs that typically (though not always) unite, rather than divide, U.S. citizens. The values are shared, though their interpretation is often contentious. There is ordinarily no left-right spectrum. Perhaps it is best called a "macro-ideology," to distinguish it from the more familiar uses of the term "ideology."

During its long annexationist phase in the nineteenth century, U.S. macro-ideology emphasized the country's identity. The goodness of its people and institutions endowed the country with a "manifest destiny" to subdue and develop a continent, wresting it if it must from Mexico, Spain, and the United Kingdom. The U.S. annexation of western North America pursued, of course, the national interests as then understood, but this act of physical expansion was clothed as well in a set of values that united U.S. citizens as they waged war to acquire territory.

As the century neared its end, the macro-ideology changed toward the external projection of the republic's values. As Secretary of State Richard Olney explained his enforcement of the Monroe Doctrine in 1895: "the people of the United States have a vital interest in the cause of popular self-government. . . . They have realized and exemplified its beneficent operation by a career unexampled in point of natural greatness or individual felicity." To defend its interests, and these values, the people of the United States "believe it not to be tolerated that the political control of an American state shall be forcibly assumed by an European power." The combination of evolving strategic interests, with the ideology of social Darwinism and the White Man's burden, endowed the United States with interests, but also with a mission, to impose order and progress on its weak southern neighbors, to force them to be free. U.S. imperialism—the indirect governance of apparently sovereign countries that were no longer annexed though were at times occupied by U.S. troops—was required by U.S. interests to keep Europe distant, and by U.S. values to keep the Americas right. As President Theodore Roosevelt told the U.S. Congress in 1905, his policies in Central America and the Latin Caribbean were "in the interest of peace as well as in the interest of justice."[2]

President Woodrow Wilson gave a more distinctly democratic cast to this enduring policy. Within a week of his inauguration, he issued a "Declaration of Policy" with regard to Latin America: "We hold . . . that just government rests always upon the consent of the governed, and that there can be no freedom without order based upon law and upon the public conscience and approval. We shall look to make these principles the basis of mutual intercourse, respect and helpfulness between our sister republics and ourselves." Wilson proceeded to be "helpful" by intervening repeatedly in Mexico, fomenting civil war to overthrow its government, sending troops to chase after Pancho Villa, and giving a new edge to Mexican fears of the United States.[3]

Beginning in the late 1920s, but more pronounced in the 1930s, the United States retreated, first, from its ideological commitment to remake the Americas in its own image and, beginning later in the 1940s, from considering the Americas essential to its national interests. The foundation of the first turning point was the memorandum prepared in 1928 by Undersecretary of State J. Reuben Clark to shape the incoming Hoover administration's Latin American policy. The Monroe Doctrine, he argued, "does not apply to purely inter-American relations. Nor does the declaration purport to lay down any principles that are to govern the interrelationship of the states of this Western Hemisphere as among themselves." Clark sought to empty the doctrine of its ideological content to emphasize national security concerns.[4] The United States may not have liked coexisting with regimes whose values it disapproved of but found it easier at last to do so.

Latin America's significance for U.S. interests was first challenged during the World War II at the very time when Latin America's military importance for the United States seemed most evident: the Americas were a bastion against the Axis powers. During World War II inter-American military relations developed and intensified.[5]

One early challenge was posed by Eugene Staley, author of the lead article in *Foreign Affairs* in April 1941. Using a geographic argument employed decades later by President Reagan for different purposes, Staley, basing himself in Madison, Wisconsin, the heartland of isolationism, wrote that "no capital in Europe, including Moscow, is as far from Madison as is Buenos Aires, and only one European capital (Athens) is as far as Rio de Janeiro." For these and other reasons, "the United States should regard western hemisphere defense lines as distinctly secondary" to Europe's.[6] Staley's view was at first quite at odds with prevailing opinion in the U.S. government about the importance of Latin America, but U.S. entry into World War II accelerated the policy change. In 1947 the editor of *Foreign Affairs* republished Staley's article in the journal's twenty-fifth anniversary volume. The article was the only one in that volume that dealt with Latin America. As Arthur Whitaker wrote: "At any time before 1941 such a proportion would have been unthinkable; since 1941 it has been about right."[7] The United States, some argued, ought to focus on Europe and on the world beyond the Americas, because Latin America mattered less and was easily defended from mainland United States.

In fact, as time passed U.S. attention to Latin America would become cyclical. It declined from the late 1940s to the late 1950s. Then it increased, thanks to the Cuban revolution and related problems, reaching a high point in the early 1960s during the Alliance for Progress. It declined again from the late 1960s to the late 1970s. Then it increased once more, thanks to revolutions in Central America, reaching a high point during the Reagan presidency. And yet even during the cycles of decreased attention, U.S. policy was concerned about the potential for revolutions linked to the USSR that might emerge from the domestic circumstances in various Latin American countries, such as Guatemala in the early 1950s and Chile in the early 1970s.

World War II's end also revived some ideological concerns. Flush from a victory as the world's "bastion of freedom," the U.S. government promoted democratic freedoms through internal interference in diverse situations, such as seeking to prevent Juan Perón's election in Argentina and democratizing Somoza's Nicaragua, mostly to no avail. The main impact of ideology's revival was on the new, formalized inter-American system.

The Inter-American Treaty of Reciprocal Assistance, signed at Rio de Janeiro in September 1947, linked democracy to collective security. According to its preamble, "the obligation of mutual assistance and common defense of the American Republics is essentially related to their democratic ideals." The treaty's article 3 committed its adherents to the view that "an armed attack by any State against an American State shall be considered as an attack against all the American States," requiring their joint assistance to the victim and resistance to the aggressor. The preamble to the Charter of the Organization of American States (OAS), signed at Bogota in May 1948, codifies the evolving ideology as well. The signers were "convinced that the historic mission of America is to offer to man a land of liberty." They were equally "confident that the true significance of American solidarity and good neighborliness can only mean the consolidation on this continent, within the framework of democratic institutions, of a system of individual liberty and social justice based on respect for the essential rights of man." Article 3 commits signatories to "representative democracy."[8]

U.S. concerns about the link between security and democracy, and about how to protect both, came together in anticommunism more strongly than in the case of earlier concerns about the extension of European influence and "systems" into the Americas. The U.S. government has been more willing to accommodate revolutions that kept some distance from potential extra-continental rivals, but revolutionary regimes found it easier to keep that distance from noncommunist powers. Fascism's appeal in the Americas, while not trivial, and stronger in some countries than in others, never rivaled the appeal of Marxism. In particular, Latin American countries, whose peoples descended from blacks and Indians as well as from southern Europeans, found it difficult to embrace Nazi Germany's Aryan racism, as did the left-wing Mexico of Lázaro Cárdenas.[9]

Marxism-Leninism combines most of the concerns that provoke condemnation, alarm, and insecurity in the United States. It is antidemocratic, antilibertarian, and anticapitalist. Embodied by the Soviet Union, the main rival to the United States since 1945, it affects human as well as property rights. Because no other earlier challenge had combined these features in the same way, it is more difficult for a Marxist-Leninist revolution to meet those significant U.S. concerns sufficiently to permit accommodation over confrontation. None ever has.

Anticommunism was included within the formal, institutionalized inter-American collective security system from its foundation. The Ninth Inter-American Conference, meeting at Bogota in April 1948, also approved unanimously a resolution on "The Preservation and Defense of Democracy in America." It declared that "by its anti-democratic nature and its interventionist tendency, the political activity of international communism or any other totalitarian doctrine is incompatible with the concept of American freedom." It stressed measures that would keep communist agents from tampering with the true will of the peoples of the Americas.[10]

The Tenth Inter-American Conference, meeting in Caracas in March 1954 as the U.S. government prepared to help to overthrow President Jacobo Arbenz in Guatemala, adopted the "Declaration of Solidarity for the Preservation of the Political Integrity of the American States against International Communist Intervention." Only Guatemala voted against it; Argentina and Mexico abstained. This Declaration reiterated its faith in "representative democracy," condemned "the activities of the international communist movement" in the Americas, declared "that the domination or control of the political institutions of any American State by the international communist movement extending to this Hemisphere the political system of an extra-continental power would constitute a threat to the sovereignty and political independence of the American States, endangering the peace of America," and expressed the "determination of the American States to take the necessary measures to protect their political independence against the intervention of international communism, acting in the interests of an alien despotism."[11] Within weeks, Arbenz fell.

In short, the United States has long been committed to a macro-ideology that has shaped its view of its national interests in a way that has profoundly influenced its policies toward its southern neighbors. After a hiatus in the 1930s, ideological concerns reappeared after the World War II and were

institutionalized in the inter-American collective security system. On the eve
of the Cuban revolution the spirit of Monroe lived. It was part of the
conceptual heritage of the Americas come alive through the collective
security instruments by the consent of their governments. There was a wide
gap between a democratic ideology and actual practice in most of Latin
America but that did not detract from the ideology's force.

The Cuban Revolution: "The System Worked"

"I don't know exactly what the difficulty is," complained President Dwight
Eisenhower at his October 28, 1959, press conference upon being asked
about relations with the revolutionary government that had come to power in
Cuba the previous January.[12] U.S.-Cuban relations had been deteriorating for
reasons that seemed incomprehensible. Cuba blamed the United States
repeatedly for acts of omission and commission. And when the United States
seemed predisposed to help, such as its readiness to discuss economic aid
during Fidel Castro's trip to the United States in April 1959, Castro requested
no aid and instructed the ministers accompanying him to engage in no such
discussions.[13]

The Cuban revolutionary government was not pushed unwillingly into
the arms of the Soviet Union, nor did the U.S. government force it to adopt
Marxism-Leninism, expropriate the means of production, repress the
opposition by means fair and foul, or found a communist regime. But the
United States did facilitate the Cuban leadership's own transformation, and
that of the revolution, in this direction. As the quotation from President
Eisenhower reveals, at first the U.S. government had no understanding of
what was going on. Once the U.S. government concluded that Cuba's was a
communist revolution aligned with the Soviet Union, President Eisenhower
(March 17, 1960) "ordered the CIA to begin to organize the training of Cuban
exiles, mainly in Guatemala."[14]

The conflict between Cuba and the United States was comprehensive.
Cuba left no U.S. policy unchallenged. Cuba aligned with the Soviet Union,
accepted its weapons and military protection, and even its ballistic missiles
and troops by the third quarter of 1962. As early as 1959, the Cuban
government, with pride, supported the overthrow of the governments of the
Dominican Republic and Nicaragua, actions that were popular because the
Trujillo and Somoza family regimes were deservedly not. Cuba expropriated
all U.S. property without compensation and refused to honor its debts to U.S.
bondholders. It installed an internal regime and designed a foreign policy that
the United States found repugnant. As a result, the internal debate in the
United States became how to be tougher on Cuba, not whether to be so. This
was best exemplified during the 1960 presidential campaign when Senator

John Kennedy conveyed the impression that Vice President Richard Nixon was insufficiently committed to the Cuban government's overthrow. Similarly, the main opponents of the Kennedy administration's Cuban policy, on the eve of the October 1962 missile crisis, criticized it for being insufficiently hard on Cuba. From mid-1960 onwards, presidential decisions to punish Cuba received strong bipartisan support.

After an inept start, U.S. policies of confrontation with Cuba were masterful in design, deeply flawed in execution, and a failure in outcome—Fidel Castro's government consolidated its rule and projected its power well beyond Cuba's boundaries. Some U.S. policies were prudent, praiseworthy, and justified; others morally damnable. They encompassed support for an exile army to overthrow the Cuban government, various plots to assassinate Fidel Castro, a trade embargo and other economic sanctions, risking nuclear war with the Soviet Union in 1962, and diplomatic efforts to isolate and punish the Cuban government. In the 1960s the collective security response was not perceived as a failure; quite the contrary it was seen as an example of how the inter-American system could work effectively to protect most of its members against one misbehaving government.

During most of 1959, Cuba outmaneuvered the United States in inter-American fora. For example, the Fifth Meeting of Consultation of the Ministers of Foreign Affairs of the American Republics was held in Santiago, Chile, in August 1959 to discuss threats to peace in the Caribbean emanating from Cuba and from the Dominican Republic. Cuba deflected attention from itself, it induced a discussion of economic issues, and it focused criticism on the Trujillo regime. By 1960, however, Cuba gave up on inter-American institutions. In February, it announced that it would not join the newly founded Inter-American Development Bank and, in March, it withdrew from the Rio Treaty.

In the summer of 1960, there were three inter-American meetings responding to a new U.S. policy. The first imposed collective sanctions on the Dominican Republic's Trujillo regime. The third approved the Act of Bogota, the forerunner of the Alliance for Progress, pledging U.S. aid for Latin American development. The second was the Sixth Meeting of Consultation of the Foreign Ministers, held at San Jose, Costa Rica. Its declaration was approved unanimously on August 29; although Cuba was not mentioned by name, its delegation walked out before the vote was taken. The declaration reaffirmed that "the inter-American system is incompatible with any form of totalitarianism" and it condemned "the intervention or the threat of intervention, even when conditional, by an extra-continental power in the affairs of the American Republics." In reply, on September 2, Fidel Castro obtained roaring approval of the "Declaration of Havana," Cuba's first call for hemispheric revolution, which also endorsed the expansion of its relations with the Soviet bloc. Cuban relations with Latin American governments deteriorated rapidly thereafter.

At Colombia's request, the Eighth Meeting of Consultation met at Punta del Este, Uruguay, in January 1962. Cuba was alone in voting against all nine resolutions. The first affirmed that "the principles of communism are incompatible with the principles of the inter-American system." The sixth specified that the "present Government of Cuba, which has officially identified itself as a Marxist-Leninist government, is incompatible with the inter-American system," and was thereby suspended from participation in it. Argentina, Bolivia, Brazil, Chile, Ecuador, and Mexico abstained on this vote. Cuba issued the Second Declaration of Havana, more militant than the first.

The missile crisis definitively turned the tide against Cuba in the inter-American system. The threat posed by Cuba was no longer in doubt. On October 22, 1962, a unanimous OAS called for the immediate dismantling and withdrawal of all Soviet missiles and other offensive weapons from Cuba and recommended that member states "take all measures individually and collectively, including the use of armed force" to achieve those aims. Venezuela and Argentina sent warships toward Cuban waters; ten other Latin American countries helped the joint military effort in some way.

In the fall of 1963 Venezuela found a large cache of weapons from Cuba intended for Venezuelan guerrillas, a finding confirmed by an OAS investigating committee. The Ninth Meeting of Consultation, meeting in Washington in July 1964, found that Cuba had committed "an aggression" against Venezuela and "an intervention" in its internal affairs. Invoking the Rio Treaty, it imposed collective sanctions on Cuba, mandating a break in diplomatic relations, the suspension of all trade with Cuba (except in foodstuffs and medicines), and of all sea transportation to or from Cuba. Bolivia, Chile, Uruguay, and Mexico voted against the resolution; the first three complied with it soon thereafter. Fidel Castro replied: "The people of Cuba will consider themselves with an equal right to help, with the resources that are available to them, the revolutionary movements in all of those countries which engage in such intervention in the internal affairs of our country."[15]

Cuba's virtually indiscriminate support for revolution and its reckless behavior in alliance with the Soviet Union had backfired. Alone in the Americas but for Mexico's cool and formal, though enduring, handshake, Cuba had to rely on communist countries for its survival. Only after 1969 did Cuban policy change enough (cutting back its support for insurgencies in Latin America) to rebuild bridges between its government and many of those in the hemisphere. Collective inter-American sanctions were lifted in 1975, although Cuba remains suspended from the system's formal institutions.

The U.S. response to the Cuban revolution achieved most of its goals except the most important: the regime did not fall. In the process the inter-

American system failed to work as a mediator for disputes among members but, instead, it worked very well as an alliance against one of its founders whose regime and policies had changed unacceptably for the other members.

In the 1960s this transformation of the inter-American system, and this use of collective security, was perceived as a great success. Most thought that the system had, in fact, "worked," because its members had agreed to act jointly against Cuba and because many of the outcomes intended by the collective policies did occur: Cuba's punishment, isolation, and condemnation. Thus the system's collective security components worked as they were designed. This very success, however, revealed the incompatibility between two of the system's central components: a mediation among members and an alliance against an enemy. The system's conciliatory and conflict resolution components had broken down.

Beyond the collective security response, it is worth recalling that the Kennedy administration's Cuban policy was faithful to the U.S. government's traditions, linking ideological and strategic issues. For example, President John Kennedy announced in his inaugural address that the United States would "pay any price, bear any burden, oppose any foe to assure the survival and the success of liberty." He proposed to "our sister republics" a new alliance for progress to enable the free governments of the Americas to cast off the chains of poverty. On the eve of the Bay of Pigs invasion, Kennedy pledged that, thanks to the Alliance for Progress, "every American Republic will be the master of its own revolution and its own hope and progress."[16] On April 3, the White House issued a "White Paper" on Cuba, written mostly by Arthur Schlesinger, Jr.: "The present situation in Cuba confronts the western hemisphere and the Inter-American system with a grave and urgent challenge . . . [and] offers a clear and present danger to the authentic and autonomous revolution of the Americas."

The U.S. and the Latin American responses to the Cuban revolution differed at the outset but soon converged. Their governments differed with Cuba in principle and in their interests. They acted jointly. Though the United States pressured and cajoled the other governments to support its views, by late 1962 and certainly by mid-1964 few had doubts that Cuba was at odds with the values that the hemisphere proclaimed—though often forgot to honor—and the interests its governments characteristically defended. There was no contradiction in the end between the U.S. and the Latin American governments in their response to the Cuban revolutionary regime.

Could this early history have been different? Many events could, of course, have intervened to change outcomes in Cuba or in its relations with the United States. Factors that suggest that the room for maneuver was modest were the historic role of the United States inside Cuba, the nature of U.S. policy, and Fidel Castro's own beliefs. A radical revolution in Cuba was likely to have come into severe conflict with the United States, considering the large U.S. political and economic role in Cuba's history. Although the U.S. role had diminished greatly on both counts, it was still substantial. The United States could have conceived of a Caribbean Yugoslavia and allowed a communist government in Havana to do internally as it pleased so long as it accepted limits on its foreign policy that met U.S. interests, but nothing in the historical record warrants this assumption, certainly not as early as in the late 1950s.

Whether a reformist revolution might have been able to live in peace with the United States is unclear. The U.S. government of the late 1950s did not look kindly on another government's restrictions on U.S. firms, much less on expropriation. The U.S. government's commitment to reforms in Latin America had yet to occur in January 1959 and would itself be, in part, a response to the Cuban revolution. The United States had accommodated revolutionary processes in Mexico and in Bolivia, but mostly when they stopped being revolutionary. In Mexico's case it took the United States decades and two world wars to recognize fully that accommodation was its best policy.

Fidel Castro was a radical, not a reformist. Everything in his biography, even accounts of the period preceding his seizing power, indicates (though it was not clear before 1959) a profound distrust for the United States, a distrust that goes well beyond Marxism-Leninism. As he put it in a private letter to his longtime associate, Celia Sánchez, six months before victory: "the Americans will pay very dearly for what they are doing." When the revolutionary war ends, he added, "a much longer and bigger war will begin for me: the war that I will make against them."[17] Or, as he told the Second Congress of the Communist party in December 1980, "The United States has been the sworn enemy of our nation" across the centuries.[18] Equally deep is his commitment to support revolutionaries elsewhere and his drive to maintain strongly centralized and uncontested power.

In short, there might have been other paths in the history of U.S.-Cuban relations that would have served them and their other neighbors better, but the political space was quite narrow already early in 1959.

The differences in U.S. and Latin American approaches toward Cuba that resurfaced in the 1970s and 1980s are beyond the scope of this chapter, but calling attention to them might help us think about the future of Nicaragua's relations with Latin America and the United States. The United States became gravely concerned about the projection of Cuban military power into Africa with the deployment of tens of thousands of combat troops in Angola and in the Horn of Africa after 1975. Latin Americans did not necessarily approve of Cuba's actions, though in some instances there was pride that a Latin American army had done so well. More importantly, Latin Americans did not think of these issues as central to their own security. The United States also remained quite concerned about the increasingly closer military collaboration between the Cubans and the Soviets in the 1970s and 1980s, a subject that the Latin Americans felt did not concern them much and was best left in U.S. hands.

Moreover, Latin American governments, one by one, came to believe that they could strike their own deal with Cuba, which at a minimum would keep Cuba from interfering in their internal affairs. In general, these deals worked, with active Cuban support for the Colombian M-19 in 1980-1981 being the main exception. The United States, in contrast, was concerned not so much about preventing Cuban interference in the United States (though this was a concern with regard to Puerto Rico) but especially about Cuba's general, worldwide policies of internationalist solidarity with revolutionary movements, which were in evidence in Cuban support for revolutions in Central America.

Latin Americans were not burdened by the history of troubled U.S.-Cuban relations. Instead, the Latin Americans found it at times helpful, and rarely incompatible with their own interests, to harness Cuba's international radicalism as one element in Latin America's own efforts to change some U.S. policies, especially on North-South international relations issues. Because the U.S. and Latin American governments came to understand that they had different interests with regard to Cuba (and with regard to many other issues), their policies toward Cuba eventually diverged.

The Nicaraguan Revolution: The System Disappeared

The values articulated by President Ronald Reagan, and the interests that his administration claimed were at stake in Nicaragua, were lineal descendants of the long history of U.S. policy toward the region. No matter how one may judge the substance of these policies, they were surely within the mainstream of a tradition committed to protect the national security and to promote liberal democracy. President Reagan eloquently articulated his government's views. His policy toward Nicaragua touched on his "most solemn duty as President. It is the cause of freedom in Central America and the national security of the United States."[19] He made those points repeatedly and linked them to his policies of isolating Nicaragua, imposing a trade embargo, mining its harbors, and supporting those who sought to overthrow its government.

During the Reagan administration, U.S. policy toward Nicaragua was stymied because many in the United States and elsewhere did not believe the president's diagnosis about, or prescription for, Nicaragua. The alternate claim was that the President's policies ill served U.S. values and interests in Nicaragua. These issues cannot be settled here, but several similarities and differences with the Cuban experience are worth highlighting.

The "objective" economic reasons for difficult relations between the

United States and Nicaragua were many fewer than in Cuba or, even earlier, in Mexico. U.S. direct investment in Nicaragua mattered little to the United States, and not much even to Nicaragua. The seizure of property belonging to the Somoza family and to their close associates in July 1979 created an economically powerful state without the need to expropriate foreign firms. Moreover, Nicaragua requested, and received, substantial U.S. aid; the United States was the leading donor to Nicaragua in 1979-1980. U.S.-supported institutions, such as the World Bank and the Inter-American Development Bank, also made large contributions to revolutionary Nicaragua. Nicaragua also honored the foreign debts that it inherited, and rescheduled them in August 1980.[20]

Until mid-1986 the Nicaraguan government did not convincingly perform the evil role assigned to it by the U.S. government. Castro's government had shut down the independent mass media and banned the opposition within eighteen months of victory; the Sandinista government shut down *La Prensa* only after seven years in power and in the midst of civil war. Also in 1986 repression intensified against Nicaragua's Roman Catholic church. But in response to the accords to promote peace and reconciliation signed in 1987 by all Central American governments at Esquipulas (at the initiative of Costa Rica's President Arias), the Nicaraguan government allowed *La Prensa* to reopen and lifted some of the restraints that had been imposed on the Roman Catholic church—a church that remains much freer than Cuba's since 1961. While the political space for opposition in Nicaragua narrowed greatly from 1981 to 1986, it remained much wider than it has been in Cuba since 1960. While in the 1980s the Nicaraguan government increased its controls over the economy, the substantial minority of the Nicaraguan economy that remained in private business hands has no parallel in post-1960 Cuba. Ten years after revolutionary victory in Nicaragua, this country's pluralism, much greater than ever existed in post-1960 Cuba, made it more difficult for the U.S. government to persuade others about its views and, in February 1990, made it possible for the legal opposition to defeat the Sandinistas in the presidential elections.

There were international differences as well. The inter-American system's formal institutions had atrophied. By the late 1970s, the system would no longer contemplate the possibility of collective peacekeeping interventions similar to those undertaken by the United Nations. As the Assistant Secretary of State for Inter-American Affairs explained to the U.S. Congress, the refusal of the OAS in June 1979 to consider sending a peace force to Nicaragua to expedite a transition from the Somoza regime to a post-Somoza regime "reflected how deeply the American states were sensitized by the Dominican intervention of 1965 and how deeply they fear physical intervention."[21] Even if the U.S. proposal to send such a force should have been rejected on its merits, the point is that a discussion on the merits became impossible because the "real issue" became U.S. intervention.

Another decisive blow to the inter-American system was the eventual U.S. government decision in 1982 to side openly with the United Kingdom in its war with Argentina over the disputed South Atlantic islands. Regardless of the merits of that case, the U.S. decision was broadly perceived in Latin America as pounding the last nail in the inter-American system's coffin. Not surprisingly, the United States did not seek the inter-American system's endorsement for its intervention in Grenada in 1983 (jointly with several English-Caribbean countries), nor did most Latin American governments endorse that action.

Notwithstanding the continued existence of the formal institutions, in practice the inter-American system ceased to exist: in the 1980s it functioned neither as a mediator between Nicaragua and the United States, nor as an alliance for one against the other. It worked neither as envisaged by its founders nor as transformed by the consent of its members (other than Cuba and Mexico) in the early 1960s. Indeed, first the Contadora process and then the Esquipulas accord emerged because the formal institutions no longer worked. Contadora and Esquipulas recaptured one of the system's original goals—mediation—that had been lost in the responses to events in Guatemala in 1954 and in Cuba after 1959.

There were, however, three key similarities between the Nicaraguan and the Cuban processes. First, there was in Sandinismo a visceral hostility toward the United States, not unlike Fidel Castro's, symbolized even in the Sandinista anthem that refers to the "Yankee, the enemy of humanity." It stemmed in part from the large U.S. role in Nicaraguan history and from the tortuous but nonetheless real ties that bound the United States and Somoza until nearly the end (with occasional exceptions), but also from the ideological convictions of key Sandinista leaders, some of whom have long been proudly and publicly Marxist-Leninists.

Second, the Nicaraguan government decided in 1980 to assist the Salvadoran insurgency by various means, including weapons. It did so despite Carter administration warnings. Nicaragua's actions were not the cause of El Salvador's troubles, though they contributed to it, but they were a key cause of the break between the Nicaraguan government and the Carter administration in its closing days. Any president of the United States would have opposed those actions. Ronald Reagan had reached his conclusions about Nicaragua even before the evidence was found, but this evidence confirmed his deeply ingrained beliefs.[22]

Third, Nicaragua drew near to the communist countries, first Cuba, and only more gradually the Soviet Union, sooner and more than was necessary or prudent, had it truly envisaged non-hostile relations with the United States. Cuban military and internal security advisers began arriving in the immediate aftermath of victory. According to the International Institute for Strategic

Studies, Soviet T-55 main battle tanks arrived in 1981, before the counterrevolutionary war had begun and before President Reagan had authorized military support for those fighting the Sandinista government (the "contras," also called the Nicaraguan Resistance). To be sure, the bulk of Soviet assistance arrived after these U.S. decisions but the latter were in part propelled by the former.[23]

It is also difficult to envisage an alternative history to Nicaragua's relations with its neighbors and with the United States. True, there was no Fidel Castro but there was a Ronald Reagan. That president's remarkably consistent views on Nicaragua stemmed above all from his ideology. That many (though not all) of the facts moved in the direction of his ideology only strengthened his views. That the ideology may have led to misguided policies that changed the facts, contrary to presumed U.S. goals, and transformed an undoubtedly difficult situation into an even more difficult one, did not seem to occur to him.

In the 1980s there was also among the Sandinistas a strong propensity toward authoritarian power (especially in 1986–1987) and toward assisting revolutionaries elsewhere. The Sandinista commitment to "internationalist solidarity" (though curtailed somewhat between 1981 and 1988) was especially strong in 1980–1981 and again in 1989, as manifested in renewed assistance to Salvadoran guerrillas. These Sandinista policies were at odds with the U.S. macro-ideology and with the values and the collective security concerns enshrined in the inter-American system's founding documents.

By 1987, fortunately, circumstances had changed in a direction that showed the enduring potential utility of collective security procedures to serve the interests of Latin American countries and of the United States. On the one hand, by the spring of 1987 renewed U.S. military support for the contras, now staffed by thousands of Nicaraguan peasants alienated from the Sandinista government, had turned the contras into a credible and effective fighting force. But rocked by the Iran-Contra scandal, the Reagan administration was much less able to continue any further its military support for the contras. On the other hand, the Sandinista government was battered by the contra war and was facing the fourth consecutive year of negative per capita income growth rates. None of the key parties could remain confident of its ability to win.

In August 1987, therefore, led by Costa Rica's President Oscar Arias, the presidents of all the Central American governments, meeting at Esquipulas in Guatemala, seized the initiative. They agreed to principles and procedures to foster internal democratization in each of the countries as a means to end the region's internal and international wars, and they also agreed to cut off support for insurgencies seeking to overthrow any of the region's governments. In the spring of 1988 negotiations between the Sandinista government and contra leaders led to a cease fire agreement at Sapoá.

Though in June 1988 these negotiations broke down, a cease fire of sorts continued to hold. Effective October 1, 1988, the U.S. Congress cut off military aid to the contras (though it continued other forms of aid). In effect, the contras had been defeated militarily. To understand why the Sandinistas won the war but lost the peace requires attention to the continued efficacy of the Esquipulas process.

The Central American presidents realized that Sandinista military victory over the Contras would not automatically bring peace much less prosperity to Nicaragua or to Central America. They continued to work with each other, focusing their pressures on Nicaragua, promising the Sandinistas eventual legitimacy if they were to hold fair elections. These time-consuming negotiations led to agreements in 1989 that set the basis for a freely contested nationwide election in Nicaragua. In the United States, the new Bush administration agreed with the U.S. Congress to cut off further military support for the contras (though continuing other forms of support). Moreover, in contrast to its predecessor, the Bush administration was prepared to allow the collective initiative of the Central American presidents to go forward in order to induce Nicaragua to abide by the policies to which it had agreed.

On February 25, 1990, a fourteen-party opposition coalition decisively defeated the Sandinistas and elected Violeta Chamorro President of Nicaragua. The U.S. government cut off all further assistance to the contras, except to ensure their repatriation and disbandment, bringing this complex episode to an end.

A Collective Security Agenda

What lessons could the hemisphere draw from its experiences with regard to Cuba and to Nicaragua for its collective security agenda? The record is clear. Except for Cuba, the Americas in 1962 unanimously opposed the deployment of Soviet strategic weapons and troops to Cuba. However, Latin America's relations with the Soviet Union became more complex since then. Several countries found that the USSR's very existence gave them room for international maneuver and even for diversifying economic relations.[24] But their own interests called for the USSR to remain unengaged militarily in the Western Hemisphere, if for no other reason than not to complicate further their relations with the United States. For comparable reasons, they no longer fear Cuba's regime and may profit from it: that Fidel Castro calls for a repudiation of the foreign debt makes everybody else look moderate and the United States more forthcoming. But there is also no support for the deployment of Cuban combat troops anywhere in the hemisphere.

Second, from the earlier formal imposition of collective sanctions on Cuba because of its support for insurgency in Venezuela to the core agenda of the Contadora and Esquipulas processes, the hemisphere's governments oppose one government's support for insurgents that seek to overthrow another. To be sure, neither the U.S. nor most Latin American and Caribbean governments have clean hands on this issue. But for the most part they understand that the collective security of all, and of each, is better served by eschewing than by promoting support for insurgencies.

No collective security system can function without adopting the second proposition and none would interest the United States without its adoption of the first proposition as well.

A key question for the U.S. and the Latin American governments will be whether the success of the Esquipulas process with regard to Nicaragua will reignite their interest in strengthening the hemisphere's collective security institutions and procedures. Will the U.S. government in the future be prepared to rely more on the slow-moving but potentially more effective and less costly collective security arrangements as means to ensure its own security and that of its Latin American neighbors? Will the Latin American governments be prepared to act collectively again to advance their self-interests, understanding that one of their interests is to make it unnecessary for the United States to act unilaterally in the Americas?

In the wake of its December 1989 invasion of Panama, the United States still seems unwilling to commit itself in advance to stop its unilateral interventions in domestic settings in the hemisphere. The U.S. government has yet to agree to procedures that would restrain its unilateral use of force in the domestic affairs of its neighboring countries. In turn, the Latin Americans have been unwilling to commit themselves in advance to support U.S. policies over security issues. The ingredients for a bargain that might reconstitute, or resurrect, a collective security system are still missing. This is regrettable at a time when democratic regimes govern most of the hemisphere's countries and when their rule has been built on the electoral defeat of political extremes to the right and to the left.

And yet the success of the Esquipulas process in 1987-1990 in Nicaragua may refocus attention on the normative value and policy utility of reliance on collective security procedures. If so, the dream that informed both James Monroe and the founders of the inter-American system—a secure America, built on freedom and democracy, which reflects the extremes that have threatened it in the past—may come closer to realization.

Notes

This chapter was commissioned by and prepared for the World Peace Foundation's project on inter-American collective security. Research on Cuba was also funded by a grant from the Ford Foundation, and general research was supported by Harvard's Center for International Affairs and Department of Government. The author bears sole

4

U.S. National Security and Latin American Revolutions: Imprismed

Robert A. Pastor

Not only have revolutions evoked similar policies from the United States and Latin American revolutionaries, they have also elicited similar questions from the United States and the Latin American public: Can the United States live with Latin American revolutions? How can events in small Latin American nations affect U.S. national security? Why does the U.S. government confront revolutionary governments when this only drives them into the arms of the Soviet Union and Cuba?

The constant repetition of these questions suggests that either simple answers are unsatisfactory, or the questions are rhetorical devices to make an ulterior point. This chapter argues that Latin American revolutionaries do pose a potential national security concern for the United States. The debate in the United States, however, has served to obscure and distort the issues rather than, for example, to clarify distinctions between security concerns and threats, or between revolutions and succession crises, or between hegemony and normal state influence. The United States and Latin American revolutionaries have been locked into a hostile, self-defeating relationship because of cross-perceptions that reinforce each other. In a sense, both sides have been imprisoned—or rather "imprismed"—by their errant, self-fulfilling preconceptions.

One of the reasons why the issue of national security and Latin American revolutions has been so clouded is simply because both terms are rarely defined, leaving the original questions imprecise, and the answers elusive. This chapter will start with definitions, and then describe and critique four separate explanations of why confrontations between the United States and revolutionaries occur. Finally, I will propose a way to avoid such confrontations in the future.

Definitions: National Security and Revolution

Few important terms are used more often and loosely and in such different contexts than the term "national security." After the Soviet Union launched

responsibility for the contents.

1. Quoted in Samuel Flagg Bemis, *The Latin American Policy of the United States* (New York: Harcourt, Brace & World, 1943), p. 64.

2. Ibid., Chapters 6 and 8; quotations from Dexter Perkins, *A History of the Monroe Doctrine* (Boston: Little, Brown, 1941), pp. 149-150, 229; Dana G. Munro, *Intervention and Dollar Diplomacy in the Caribbean, 1900-1921* (Princeton, New Jersey: Princeton University Press, 1964).

3. Bemis, *The Latin American Policy*, Chapters 6 and 8; Howard F. Cline, *The United States and Mexico*, rev. ed. (New York: Atheneum, 1965); quotation from Bemis, *The Latin American Policy*, p. 175.

4. Quoted in Perkins, *A History of the Monroe Doctrine*, p. 342. See also Bryce Wood, *The Making of the Good Neighbor Policy* (New York: Columbia University Press, 1961).

5. Jack Child, *Unequal Alliance: The Inter-American Military System, 1938-1978* (Boulder: Westview Press, 1980), Chapters 2-4.

6. Eugene Staley, "The Myth of the Continents," *Foreign Affairs* 19 (1941): 481-494.

7. Arthur P. Whitaker, *The Western Hemisphere Idea* (Ithaca: Cornell University Press, 1954), pp. 161-164.

8. Texts in U.S. Congress, House Committee on Foreign Affairs, *Inter-American Relations*, 93rd Cong., 1st. sess., 1973.

9. See Cole Blasier, *The Hovering Giant: U.S. Responses to Revolutionary Change in Latin America, 1910-1985*, rev. ed. (Pittsburgh: University of Pittsburgh Press, 1985).

10. See J. Lloyd Mecham, *The United States and Inter-American Security, 1889-1960* (Austin: University of Texas Press, 1961), p. 429.

11. House Committee on Foreign Affairs, *Inter-American Relations*, pp. 199-200.

12. U.S. Department of State, *American Foreign Policy: Current Documents, 1959* (Washington, D.C.: GPO, 1959), document 101.

13. Jorge I. Domínguez, *Cuba: Order and Revolution* (Cambridge: Harvard University Press, 1978), pp. 139-164.

14. Dwight D. Eisenhower, *Waging Peace* (Garden City, New York: Doubleday, 1965), p. 524.

15. Texts of inter-American resolutions in House Committee on Foreign Affairs, *Inter-American Relations*, pp. 202-203, 227-232, 235, and in *Current Documents, 1962*, document 59; Cuban materials in *Revolución* July 30-August 10, 1959; ibid., February 5, 1960, p. 14; ibid., March 29, 1960, p. 6; September 3, 1960, p. 1; and *Obra revolucionaria*, no. 18 (1964), p. 30.

16. U.S. Department of State, *Current Documents*, 1961, document 132.

17. Cited in Alexandr Alexeev, "Cuba después del triunfo de la revolución. Primera parte," *América latina*, no. 10 (October 1984): 63.

18. *Granma Weekly Review*, December 28, 1980, p. 13.

19. U.S. Department of State, Bureau of Public Affairs, *Current Policy* 850 (June 24, 1986), p. 1.

20. Arturo Cruz Sequeira, "Nicaragua: crisis económica, radicalización o moderación?" in *Centroamérica: más allá de la crisis* (Mexico: Ediciones SIAP, 1983), pp. 148-149; John Purcell, "The Interests and Perceptions of U.S. Business in Relation to the Political Crisis in Central America" (Paper presented at a workshop titled "The International Aspects of the Crisis in Central America" at the Woodrow Wilson Center for Scholars, Washington, D.C., April 1981).

21. Viron P. Vaky, "Statement before the Subcommittee on Inter-American Affairs, Committee on Foreign Affairs, U.S. House of Representatives," June 26,

1979, p. 11.
    22. The best single source on Nicaragua's actions in 1980-1981 remains U.S. Department of State, *Communist Interference in El Salvador: Documents Demonstrating Communist Support of the Salvadoran Insurgency* (Washington, D.C.: February 23, 1981). The "White Paper" to which the documents were appended has been rightly criticized for inaccuracies and exaggeration. The documents do not support several of the White Paper's key assertions. However, the authenticity of the documents remains unchallenged, and they do support the proposition that Nicaragua contributed many resources to the Salvadoran insurgency in 1980-1981.
    23. Theodore Schwab and Harold Sims, "Relations with the Communist States," in *Nicaragua: The First Five Years,* ed., Thomas Walker (New York: Praeger, 1985).
    24. Cole Blasier, *The Giant's Rival: The USSR and Latin America* (Pittsburgh: University of Pittsburgh Press, 1983).

Sputnik, President Eisenhower judged that U.S. national security depended on educating a new generation of Americans in science, and Congress passed the National Defense Education Act. President Kennedy implored Congress to pass the Trade Expansion Act of 1962 in the name of national security. President Johnson sent U.S. citizens to fight in Vietnam in the interest of U.S. national security, and President Nixon withdrew them for the same reason. Nixon first used "national security" as a defense against Watergate, while Carter used it to advance his national energy program. President Reagan frequently invoked the term to persuade Congress to give aid to the contras. Any term used to guide the United States through so many different problems should raise eyebrows and questions.

    The simplest definition of "national security" is the "defense of a nation's interests and values," but such a definition begs more questions than it answers. What is the nation? How do you define its interests or values? Is it territory, property, the economy, values, or its future (destiny)? If values or property, does that include the "human rights" of foreigners or the overseas property of U.S. citizens? Who is to decide? What is the best response to a national security problem or threat?

Which Interests?

Do national interests include strategic interests in defending the United States against Soviet missiles, geopolitical interests in maintaining alliances, the political interest of the president, the economic interests of the large or small businessmen, or the environmental interests of the larger community or the Sierra Club?

Who Decides Which Interests Should Be Given Priority?

Nations can seldom, if ever, pursue all their interests at the same time; thus decisions need to be made between which interests should be merely pursued (trade-offs) and which come first (priorities). This raises the question as to who decides, and which decisions count as national commitments. For the United States, the president is commander in chief, but Congress shares with the Executive Branch the powers to make treaties, appropriate money for defense, and appoint ambassadors. Within the Executive Branch, the Secretaries of State and Defense and the National Security Advisor often vie for the right to make policy. How does one weigh the statements by an Assistant Secretary of State if Congress passes a resolution contradicting his position?

When Is the Best Time to Respond, and What Is the Best Defense of a Nation?

When does a potential threat require a response? Should force be a first option or a last resort in dealing with a threat to national security? Do troops on the border provide the best defense, or is the best defense, as Vince Lombardi used to say, a good offense?

U.S. history has not provided a single set of answers to these three basic questions of national security: (1) which interests? (2) who decides on priority? and (3) when and how to respond? Rather, U.S. national security policy is replete with examples of diverse interests, shifting priorities, different decisionmakers, and widely varying responses. However, with some exceptions, one trend has been the steady expansion of our nation's conception of its national security.

In the eighteenth century after the Treaty of Paris, the United States was compelled to send troops to its frontiers in response to covert efforts by Great Britain, Spain, and the Indians conspiring to destabilize the young country. By 1819, with its borders more secure, the United States judged that the best defense was to acquire contiguous territory, and it purchased Florida and soon embarked on its western expansion. In 1823, the United States decided that its security depended on excluding Europe from establishing new colonies in the hemisphere. During the period of the country's worst internal division—the Civil War—both the Union and the Confederacy asked foreign powers for aid, much as many divided Latin American governments would later invite the United States and other powers.

In the nineteenth century, the United States, by and large, ignored the chronic instability in the Caribbean basin. In the twentieth century, after investing in a canal in Panama, the United States became preoccupied with the region's instability, lest other foreign powers gain a foothold in the region and endanger the new U.S. asset.

Still, there were many different ways to defend the canal and U.S. interests in Latin America during the twentieth century. Theodore Roosevelt and his Secretary of State Elihu Root tried to preclude instability by international treaties. William Howard Taft used marines, dollars, and customs receiverships. Woodrow Wilson replaced "dollar diplomacy" with the promotion of democracy, but he continued to use the marines. Franklin D. Roosevelt pledged nonintervention and meant it. Truman and Carter tried, but failed, to encourage two different Somozas to give up power, while Eisenhower and Nixon sent ambassadors to Nicaragua that considered U.S. interests as identical with those of the Somozas. In short, U.S. presidents not only defined interests differently, but they also chose different means to defend them.

Since independence, the United States has never felt completely secure in Latin America for very long. One scholar has described this as "national insecurity,"[1] implying that it stems from either a hegemonic impulse or some psychological malady, but as Thomas Hobbes noted, "national insecurity" is the natural state of international relations. As there is no international monopoly on the use of force, all nations will always be insecure. The only ways to guarantee security are to eliminate one's neighbors, keep them weak, or prevent them from being used by a more powerful rival. Short of these conditions, the United States cannot escape from the security dilemma. The questions then return: How to define security? How to defend it?

In his search for a definition of "national security" and some guidance as to when it is in jeopardy, Arnold Wolfers concluded that it is little more than an "ambiguous symbol" used by presidents to build support for a particular program.[2] In the United States, everyone can define security differently, but only the president is elected by all the people to take the responsibility to define and defend the nation's interests. As we have seen, each president will employ the term "national security" to try to gain support for his policy. Ironically, the term is invoked less in those cases where the threat to national security is self-evident—for example, after Pearl Harbor or the installation of Soviet missiles in Cuba—than where the connection is more tenuous or debatable—for example, in the Panama Canal Treaties or aid to the Contras. The public opposed the treaties and the Contras, and so Carter and then Reagan felt compelled often to invoke the term "national security" to secure congressional approval of each.

Rather than a guide, "national security" is a concept that is subjective, relative, and dynamic. It is subjective because it depends on the personality and bureaucratic role of the definer. A conservative president is likely to interpret threats to the United States more intensely than a liberal, and the Pentagon will always describe threats in more ominous terms than the Department of State.

A country that is threatened is like a person under stress; it is likely to see the external threat as more serious and imminent than someone who is relaxed and has calm, friendly relations with his neighbor. In other words, the sense of threat depends on the times and the external and internal environment.

The concept is relative. How a country's leaders define their nation's security depends on the size, power, and self-concept of a country. Small, poor, divided countries are more likely to be preoccupied with internal threats, but paradoxically, the larger and richer countries are more likely to spend more money on defense. It is not surprising that when oil revenues multiplied in 1979, Venezuela and Mexico began defining their national security in more expansive and international terms. Threats to these countries had not diminished after 1982, but their policies became less active and external because their resources and capabilities declined with the price of oil and the rise in debt.

Finally, the concept of "national security" is dynamic. The history of the United States illustrates how its definition of national security expanded with its economy, wealth, and power. Richer people in exclusive neighborhoods are not threatened more by crime than poor people in the ghettos. The rich have more locks on their doors because they can afford more.

There is, in brief, no single or simple formula for defining a nation's security or judging when it is at risk. If there were such a formula, one wouldn't need a government. National security policy could be made by computer. But without a formula, *one needs to make judgments of the nature and immediacy of a threat. On this, people naturally differ.*

There is also no simple prescription for the best defense or any obvious reason why revolutions in small countries in the Caribbean basin should threaten the national security of the United States. The next step, then, is to define "revolution."

Walter LaFeber defines "revolution" as "virtually the only method of transferring power" in Central America, and thus comparable to elections in the United States.[3] LaFeber's thesis is that the United States opposes all revolutions, but his definition would include every coup d'état in the region—most of which the United States accepted, and some of which it encouraged.

An alternative definition of "revolution" would be as a purposive, violent, and fundamental change in society in which power is transferred across social classes, or rather from one elite, representing the middle or upper classes, to another, oriented toward a lower class.[4] Using this definition, there have been only three genuine revolutions in the Western Hemisphere: Mexico, Cuba, and Nicaragua. Revolutions are not inevitable; they are exceptional.

Moreover, it is significant that these three great Latin American revolutions began as crises of political succession, and only succeeded because the nation rose up to depose a hated dictator. In these cases, the revolutionaries promised free elections, the middle class backed the revolution, and the United States withdrew its support from the dictator at a crucial moment. *Thus, in the only cases when genuine revolutions occurred in the Caribbean basin, the United States did not actively oppose the revolutionaries.*

Despite the conventional wisdom, the United States has not always opposed revolutionaries or even revolutionary governments, and it has not always supported right-wing dictators. The United States withdrew support from Batista in 1958 and from the Somozas in 1947 and 1977. Indeed, the United States initially tried to forge friendly and respectful relationships with the Cuban and Nicaraguan revolutions; the confrontation that occurred in these two cases was predictable but not inevitable.

Still, it is accurate to say that generally the United States has pursued a hostile policy toward leftist revolutionaries and leftist revolutionary governments. Why? In the next sections, we shall identify, describe, and evaluate four sets of explanations:

1. The revolutionary perspective: the United States confronts revolutions because they are threats to world capitalism.
2. The hegemonic theory: the United States confronts revolutions because they are threats to the U.S. sphere of influence.
3. The conventional national security approach: the United States confronts leftist revolutions because they represent an expansion of the Soviet empire.
4. The indirect security perspective: the United States confronts Marxist-Leninist revolutionaries because their ties to the Soviet Union and Cuba make them indirect threats to U.S. interests.

The revolutionary and conventional security explanations describe revolutions as direct threats to U.S. national security, albeit for very different reasons. The hegemonic thesis is different from the others in that it is more of a critique of hegemony than an explanation of it; it suggests that revolutions constitute no threat to U.S. national security. The indirect security explanation views revolutions as potential or indirect threats. The first and second explanations agree, albeit for very different reasons, that the United States should accept revolutions; while the third and the fourth believe that U.S. interests require a response.

Table 4.1   Approaches to Revolution: Four Explanations

| | | Threats to National Security | |
		Direct	Indirect or None
U.S.	Accept	Revolutionary	Hegemonic
Responses	Don't Accept	National Security	Indirect

Motives for Confrontation

The Revolutionary Interpretation

To Fidel Castro, the reason for the confrontation between Cuba and the United States is simple: "The United States is responsible . . . It has never wanted to accept the existence of the Cuban revolution or the establishment of a social system that is different from its own."[5]

Maurice Bishop, the Prime Minister of revolutionary Grenada from 1979 to 1983 offered his views of U.S. belligerence:

> From the first days of coming to power [by the New Jewel Movement], the
> United States pursued a policy, which showed no respect for our national
> pride and aspirations, and sought constantly to bring the Revolution to its
> knees . . . On reflection and analysis, we conclude that such an attitude [by
> the United States] exists principally *because Grenada has taken a very*
> *decisive and firm step on the road to genuine national independence*, non-
> alignment, and self-determination.[6] (Emphasis added.)

Why did the United States confront revolutionary Nicaragua? Jaime
Wheelock, one of the nine members of the Sandinista Directorate, explained:

> We are a danger for the United States; not only because we are a country
> with an independent foreign policy that it considers negative for its interests,
> . . . but fundamentally *because we represent the shattering of its classic*
> *model of domination for Latin America* . . . In reality, we are carrying out
> for the first time in Central America what the United States and its model
> always promised the people. Under revolutionary hegemony, we are
> attaining peace, stability, progress for the people, and a more perfect
> democracy . . . A rupture of this classic model has global effects, for this
> North American model is in crisis, is being broken.[7] (Emphasis added.)

There are several consistent threads that connect these three views of
U.S. policy. First, the United States cannot tolerate "independent" behavior
by Third World nations. Secondly, the United States cannot accept social
change in the Third World. A third element, but one only implicit in these
three quotes, is that U.S. corporations and the capitalist system define and
direct U.S. policy. Revolutions are aimed to liberate the people from
capitalists, and thus, revolutions, as Wheelock said, threaten the core of the
oppressive system maintained by U.S. "imperialism." According to this
interpretation, revolutions constitute a national security threat to the United
States, which logically should try to prevent revolutions.

Let's examine each of these premises in reverse order:

1. That U.S. security interests are indistinguishable from U.S. corporate
interests in the Third World. Up until the revolutions in Nicaragua, Grenada,
and El Salvador, the confrontation with the U.S. government was almost
always preceded by a clash with U.S. business interests. From this pattern,
some concluded that the relationship between the U.S. government and U.S.
business was direct and causal, with the latter directing the former. This,
however, has almost never been the case.

During those periods when U.S. policy has encouraged U.S. investment
abroad, the primary motive has been to assist those countries whose
instability were sources of national security concern to the United States.

Businessmen were naturally reluctant to invest in such unstable areas, and the government often had to apply pressures or devise incentives to encourage them. Even then, businessmen did not always respond. President Ronald Reagan's largely unproductive effort to stimulate investment in Jamaica is just the most recent case.

The crucial issue, however, is not so much whether the U.S. government promotes foreign investment, but whether the government will always defend U.S. businesses that are threatened. In two pivotal investment disputes—Mexico's oil nationalization in 1938 and Guatemala's expropriation of United Fruit Company land in 1952—the U.S. government distinguished between business and national interests and gave the latter priority. President Roosevelt refused to support the oil companies in Mexico, adopting a patient and farsighted approach. In Guatemala, the United States adopted a shortsighted policy, aimed at overthrowing the Arbenz regime, but the principal motive was the perception of increasing Soviet influence. After the coup, the Justice Department disassembled United Fruit by an antitrust suit, "breaking up the firm's banana business and ending its role in Guatemala,"[8] more completely than Arbenz had envisaged.

The argument that U.S. business runs the State Department has been rendered even less convincing as a result of some fundamental changes that have occurred since the mid-1970s.[9] First, U.S. corporations have largely abandoned the natural resource and communications sectors, primarily because of nationalizations. At the same time, a large proportion of U.S. direct investment shifted from Latin America to more secure sites in Europe and Canada. Secondly, by the late 1970s, most Latin American governments, including the government of Cuba, were eagerly soliciting foreign investment. Third, by the 1980s, the Nicaraguan and Grenadian revolutions pledged to respect a mixed economy, and Nicaragua went to great pains to reschedule rather than repudiate its debt. Today, U.S. businesses have fewer interests in Latin America, and the U.S. government is more removed from them.

A more sophisticated radical interpretation of U.S. policy would argue that the United States opposes revolutions because it wants to preserve the position of U.S. investment in the future. Again, this interpretation tends to overlook the reduced importance of the region for U.S. business and the increased interest of socialist and communist countries in U.S. trade and investment.

2. That the U.S. opposes social change in Latin America. This charge draws from the experience of U.S. hostility to the governments in Guatemala (1951-1954), Cuba (1959-1961), and Chile (1970-1973). However, in each of these cases, the United States concentrated its attention on the ties between the revolutionary leaders and the Soviet Union. In the democratic revolutions in

Bolivia in the 1950s, Venezuela during the 1960s, and El Salvador during the late 1970s and early 1980s, the United States supported social reforms. Moreover, by its aid program and contributions to the multilateral development banks, the United States has provided a powerful stimulus to economic development and social change.

Some argue that revolutions are born of poverty and social injustice, and they therefore equate U.S. hostility to revolutions with opposition to social change. This assertion suffers from two flaws. First, it is debatable whether the social changes that follow from violent revolution are more enduring and important than those that follow from gradual, peaceful change—the kind that the United States prefers. The Mexican revolution was so devastating that it took the country thirty years before the economy was restored to where it had been *before* the revolution. Similarly, in Nicaragua, one decade after the revolution, the per capita gross domestic product was less than half of what it had been *before* the revolution.[10]

Secondly, revolutions in Latin America—whether in Mexico, Cuba, or Nicaragua—have been less the product of economic stagnation and injustice than of dramatic economic and social progress within an anachronistic political system. The origin of revolution has not been the absence of change, but the unevenness of change. And the leaders—whether Francisco Madero, Fidel Castro, or Carlos Fonseca Amador—were children of the middle class, not the working class or the peasantry.

3. *That the United States opposes independent policies.* The United States opposed the Cuban, Grenadian, and Nicaraguan revolutions not because they were *nonaligned*, but because they were *aligned*, or perceived to be aligned, with the Soviet Union. The United States has not opposed the other Latin American and Caribbean governments that participate in the Non-Aligned Movement (NAM). During the Carter administration, the United States encouraged Latin American governments to join the NAM. Moreover, to suggest that the United States opposed these revolutions because of their independence is to suggest that Mexico, Venezuela, Jamaica, Peru, Brazil, and Argentina are subservient to the United States.

The idea the the United States opposes revolutions in Latin America because it fears that the capitalistic system would collapse if they succeeded is fanciful. If Cuba pursued the logic of its position that economic relations with the United States is inherently exploitative, then it would seek an embargo on trade with the United States rather than try to remove it.

The United States has often confronted both revolutionaries and revolutionary governments, but the explanations offered by revolutionaries are not convincing. Historically, the United States has opposed some social changes; it has defended some businesses abroad, and it has become frustrated, even angry, at some independent foreign policies. But at other times, the United States has been a firm supporter of social change; it has ignored or rejected protests by U.S. business; and it has been willing to listen, accept, and sometimes even adjust to Latin American criticism. It is clear that other factors are more important in explaining U.S. policy than these.

The continuing belief by revolutionaries that the United States opposes social change and independent policies and unequivocally defends business is more of an explanation of why revolutionaries continue to confront the United States than it is an explanation of U.S. policy. Like those who believe in the "national security" interpretation, revolutionaries believe that revolutions are a threat to the United States, and therefore do not expect it to accept revolutions and would interpret acceptance as a sign of the objective weakening of U.S. imperialism.

The Hegemonic Interpretation

The Hegemonic Interpretation is a variation on one element of the radical argument. Keohane and Nye defined "hegemony" as when "one state is powerful enough to maintain the essential rules governing interstate relations, and willing to do so."[11] The hegemonic perspective suggests that the United States confronts revolutions because they challenge its right or ability to set the rules. Those who employ this line of argument tend to be critical of the U.S. government's "hegemonic presumption," that "the entire hemisphere was a rightful sphere of U.S. influence."[12] *Thus, the hegemonic interpretation is actually an antihegemonic prescription.* The United States confronts revolutions because it won't accept independent deviations from the U.S. "sphere of influence." The problem is "in the minds" of U.S. policymakers.[13]

The implication of this line of argument is that the United States ought to see revolutions not as security threats but as challenges to U.S. dominance or political preeminence and, therefore, to be more relaxed about them.[14] From this perspective, the greatest threat to U.S. interests would be to try to prevent this natural evolution toward national dignity. Jose Lopez Portillo, the former president of Mexico articulated this viewpoint in an address on February 21, 1982:

> I can assure my good friends in the United States that what is taking place here in Nicaragua, what is taking place in El Salvador, and what is blowing throughout the whole region, does not constitute an intolerable danger to the basic interests and the national security of the United States. What does constitute a danger [for the United States] is the risk of history's condemnation as a result of suppressing by force the rights of other nations.

The hegemonic interpretation yields a compelling insight, the nationalist motive of revolutions in the Caribbean basin, but it also contains a number of serious problems. First, the hegemonic critique of U.S. policy implies that there is a qualitative difference between hegemonic and normal state influence, rather than just a quantitative difference. In other words, it suggests that the exercise of U.S. influence in the region is driven by some peculiar national psychic malady to dominate rather than the normal interests of a nation.

All nations, whether large or small, seek to influence their neighbors' internal politics and external policies. European political parties support their Christian and Social Democratic counterparts like the Communists do because they prefer like-minded parties in power. Even Mexico, which routinely condemns intervention and defends self-determination, has recognized that internal developments within Guatemala can affect Mexico, and it has therefore actively sought to prevent Guatemala from swinging to either extreme, left or right.[15]

The two key distinctions between the policies of the United States and these other countries or groups are *national styles* and *capabilities*. For reasons having to do with its national self-image, the United States shapes and justifies its exercise of power by reference to moral considerations, and policy has always reflected a unique mixture of idealism and realism. The more important distinction, however, is based on the differences in power. When Mexico was wealthy in its oil-boom honeymoon of 1978 to 1982, it intervened more in Central America to pursue its interests. When it was in debt and self-preoccupied before and after that, it had fewer resources with which to extend its influence. Its objectives had not changed; its interests in shaping the region in ways compatible with its goals had not changed; what changed was its capability. To a great degree, the reach of the United States into the region's internal affairs is the result of the expansion of U.S. capabilities. Of course, influence can be and has been exercised in many different ways.

Second, the hegemonic approach implies that the ideological ties of nationalistic revolutions or the character of a regime ought not to concern the United States, or at least ought not to justify U.S. opposition. According to this view, U.S. opposition pushes revolutions toward the Soviet Union, and a passive policy would not. But this underestimates the depth of the ideological commitment of revolutionaries and overestimates the degree to which their approach is simply a reaction to U.S. policy. Most revolutionaries routinely define the United States as their enemy. Why should the United States help or even facilitate the success of a group that views it as an enemy just because that group claims that it is fighting for social justice?

Third, the hegemonic interpretation overestimates the rigidity in the inter-American system. The history of the Caribbean basin in the twentieth century can be viewed as a continuous redefinition of the bounds of legitimate influence by the United States. Put a different way, the nations of the region have gradually but inexorably extended the boundaries of their autonomy and, with a few exceptions, reduced the degree and kinds of physical coercion exercised by foreign powers. The United States initially used marines to determine both internal and external policies, but gradually it was impelled to focus its interests and limit its coercion. The advance of civilization is the tightening of constraints against physical coercion. This does not mean that force is obsolete; it will remain the ultimate instrument as long as there are nation-states, but force is now more costly and thus less useful.

Some suggest that the best approach for the United States toward revolutions is to be helpful and supportive and try to co-opt revolutionaries. U.S. policies can make revolutionaries either much more or a little less hostile, but the probabilities argue against converting Marxist-Leninist guerrillas, who have been fighting U.S. imperialism for a decade or so, into either democrats or friends of the United States.

This is not to suggest that the hegemonic interpretation is without any foundation or utility. On the contrary, its stress on the psychological and political motives of U.S. policymakers represents a valuable contribution to the discussion on national security. Its flaw is the disproportionate weight it gives to these motives, suggesting that the "national security" concerns of U.S. policymakers are either a projection of a distorted U.S. mindset or a deliberate public relations exercise to gather public support for a policy of dominance.

The Security Interpretation

While the hegemonic perspective minimizes the possibility of any real threat to U.S. interests in the region, the national security approach sees threats intensely and everywhere. Two simple premises underlie the national security interpretation: First, U.S. national security interests are directly threatened by Marxist revolutionaries and regimes. Second, the United States should use "all means necessary" to prevent Marxists from coming to power or from consolidating their regimes.

While the United States opposes Marxism-Leninism globally, it has been especially vigorous in preventing revolution in the Caribbean basin because of three factors: the proximity to the U.S.; the vulnerability of the small open nations of the region to instability; and the historical role of the United States and its continuing large influence, which often impel revolutionaries to identify the United States as their enemy and to seek support from the enemies of the United States—Cuba and the Soviet Union. Marxist revolutions in Africa have therefore stirred considerably less interest in the United States than revolutions in Latin America.

In reviewing the litany of national security interests, policymakers generally begin by mentioning access to strategic minerals. Leaving aside for the moment the relative dearth of non-substitutable strategic minerals in the Caribbean basin, the entire question has been turned on its head by Third World nationalizations of natural resource industries in the 1960s and 1970s. Provided that the United States continues to accept the principle of sovereignty over natural resources, it is hard to conceive that a county would not want to sell its minerals to the United States. The only impediment to Cuba's nickel exports to the United States is the U.S. embargo. In brief, changes in the world have made a prior U.S. concern with access to minerals less important than the contemporary concerns of developing countries for access to U.S. markets. Because of stockpiles and fabricated substitutes, these concerns are unlikely to be inverted even during a war.

A more important security interest is access to strategic sealanes of communication (SLOCs). Michael Desch offers a cogent argument on the significance of the sealanes by focusing on the impact of Soviet bases or its fleet in the region in the case of a major U.S.-Soviet war in Europe, admittedly the principal U.S. strategic interest.[16] Reinforced by a credible Cuban military capability, such forces could tie down the United States for a critical period. The United States could cope with the threat, but it would be a major undertaking—he argues that it would require more than 600 aircraft—and could seriously hamper the ability to reinforce our European allies.

During World War II, without any bases in the Caribbean, and with a smaller, more primitive submarine fleet than the Soviet's today, the German navy wreaked havoc on Allied shipping in the region. There is little reason to doubt that if a war between the United States and the Soviet Union remained conventional for an extended period, the Soviets would have similar success paralyzing United States and Allied shipping. But it is not clear that they need Cuba, and indeed, one could argue that the Cubans would have a compelling reason not to be used. During the last thirty years, the United States has often looked for pretexts to punish the Castro regime. If Cuba or any other country in the region were to interfere with U.S. shipping, that would constitute a legitimate justification for action, not just a pretext. Indeed, after identifying the sealanes threat to the United States, Desch's prescription for dealing with it is a deterrent posture based on threats of nuclear retaliation.

In brief, the Soviets have ample naval capability without the need for Cuban naval bases, and small nations in the region have a vital security interest to avoid war against the United States and not be used for that purpose. Therefore, it is hard to see how the sealanes could be threatened by revolution in Central America.

Another concern stems from the threat of subversion. A revolutionary regime could undermine or overthrow its neighbors, forcing the United States to divert scarce resources to continental defense. To suggest, however, that a Marxist Nicaragua would require the permanent deployment of sizable numbers of U.S. forces on its border is to forget that there are four countries between Nicaragua and the border, and that there are many more efficient and effective ways to deter or respond to Nicaraguan expansion. If Nicaragua were to invade its neighbors or expand its support for insurgencies, the best response would be collective and the best vehicle would be the OAS or a group of concerned countries.

Perhaps the most important factor is the belief that security is indivisible. President Reagan underscored the centrality of this point in his speech before a Joint Session of Congress on April 27, 1983: "If we cannot defend ourselves [in Central America], we cannot expect to prevail elsewhere. Our credibility would collapse, our alliances would crumble, and the safety of our homeland would be put at jeopardy." While some Europeans might see NATO's future as connected to that of Central America, as President Reagan did, the dominant view in Europe would probably be one of bewilderment over the U.S. obsession with the region.

Besides Alliance perceptions, an additional U.S. security concern has been that the countries of the region are vulnerable—like dominoes—to the subversion and expansionism of Nicaragua. While it is true that events in one country in the region affect the others, there is no direct, automatic, or inevitable effect, and it is inaccurate to suggest that they would fall like dominoes. The experience of the years since the Nicaraguan revolution suggest that the opposite is more nearly the case. Since 1979, the right and the center in Central America have been strengthened much more than the left.

Though the arguments advanced on behalf of the national security perspective—like those of the revolutionary perspective—are thin, they have weighty consequences. A logic connects the definition of interests with the perception of the threat and the prescription. If one accepted the description of U.S. interests in Central America as vital and saw the Nicaraguan threat as direct, then the United States should have used "all means necessary" to remove the threat and change the regime. The costs of such an approach would have exceeded the possible benefits and, indeed, the fact that Reagan did not escalate the war to the point of direct U.S. military involvement suggests that he accepted this cost/benefit calculation, despite his rhetoric.

Nonetheless, a president pays a political price for maintaining such a wide discrepancy between rhetoric and policy for a prolonged period. Reagan was able to avoid this problem because most U.S. politicians feared that he meant what he said about eliminating the Sandinistas; they therefore tried to restrain him. The opposite, however, occurred with President George Bush. When a gap opened between Bush's rhetorical attacks on General Manuel Antonio Noriega of Panama and his policies, congressional critics accused him of timidity. Congress, in effect, stopped holding back the president and began pushing him toward military action. In brief, there are serious consequences when a president characterizes a threat as direct or our vital interests as being engaged; this need not lead automatically to military action, but the probability of that occurring increases.

Indirect Security Perspective

Much as the hegemonic interpretation extracts and elaborates the most convincing element of the revolutionary view, the indirect security perspective offers a more sophisticated variation on the national security view. According to this approach, revolutions *can* conceivably pose a threat to the United States, but it is indirect and the nations of the region are affected more than the United States. The proper response by the United States should be limited and proportional to the nature of the threat. Bertrand Russell offered the rationale for proportional response:

> Resistance, if it is to be effective in preventing the spread of evil, should be combined with the greatest degree of understanding and the smallest degree of force that is compatible with the survival of the good things we wish to preserve.[17]

The underlying premise of the indirect security perspective is different from that of the security or hegemonic perspectives. The security perspective views the problem as stemming from Soviet penetration while the hegemonic views it as stemming from indigenous sources of instability. The indirect security perspective agrees with the security view that the external and internal problems are connected, but it disagrees on the direction of causality, believing that, more often than not, it is the revolutionary group that *invites* the foreign rival rather than the foreign rival that *directs* the revolutionary group. More importantly, the indirect approach does not view the connection as unbreakable or certain, but rather as probable. In other words, under conditions of revolutionary turmoil, the probability is that revolutionary groups will turn for help to the Soviets or the Cubans, but that is neither inevitable nor certain.

The indirect perspective is concerned with three security interests: a military relationship with the Soviet Union and Cuba; support for subversion; and as a catalyst for anti-U.S. activities. These interests are related but distinct.

Once a revolutionary, anti-U.S. group takes power, it can legally invite a powerful, hostile government like the Soviet Union to defend it or to help expand its influence. Why would a guerrilla group motivated by an interest in self-determination seek help from the Soviet Union or Cuba? For two reasons: first, Marxist-Leninist groups are, by their self-definition, oriented toward the Soviet Union and Cuba; they have tended to believe that these governments have answers, which are relevant to their national experience, while also believing that U.S. imperialism is their problem. If the Soviet Union itself turns inward, then its relationship with revolutionary groups will change as well.

Secondly, Marxist-Leninist groups tend to believe that the United States will try to destroy their revolution, and therefore, they seek powerful friends to deter the United States or to help them obtain the means to defend themselves. Thus, during the first moments of the Grenadian and Nicaraguan revolutions, in spite of the fact that U.S. policy was supportive or neutral, the revolutionary groups turned to Cuba and the Soviet Union for military aid. As U.S. policy changed from trying to relate to the revolution to trying to undermine it, the revolutionary governments deepened their military relationships with the Soviet Union and Cuba. This, in turn, prompted the United States to harden its approach. As the relationship deteriorated, the revolutionary governments had additional incentives to invite the enemies of the United States to try to defend it—either by establishing a base or providing more arms.

As revolutionaries, the new leaders also tend to believe that a good way to deter the United States is to encourage revolutions elsewhere. Of course, such tactics have the opposite effect on the United States, where leaders conclude that the revolutionaries cannot be trusted. And as denunciations are exchanged, the United States finds itself in a confrontation with a small government, which looks heroic while the United States looks foolish.

The U.S. government has long believed that its influence is greater, and the risks to world peace are fewer, in preventing a hostile group from coming to power than in preventing a hostile government from asking the Soviet Union for help. The difficulty for U.S. policymakers is compounded when the revolutionary group either disguises its intentions or has diverse, complicated, or obscure goals. The eventual confirmation of the initial suspicions of the United States about the radical, Marxist-Leninist tendencies of the three groups—the 26th of July Movement, the New Jewel Movement, and the Sandinista Front—doubtlessly will influence future perceptions. And the same is true from the other direction: the worst fears of these three groups about U.S. intolerance were also confirmed, and future revolutionary groups may be less interested in negotiating a modus vivendi with the United States.

Is such a confrontation inevitable? If the United States did not adopt a hostile approach to the revolutionary regime, would it have deepened its military relationship with the Soviet Union or Cuba? In the two recent cases of Nicaragua and Grenada, the revolutionaries turned to Cuba for a military relationship, even while the United States was offering help. When U.S. policy became more distant or hostile, the two revolutionary governments deepened and accelerated their militarization, became more dependent on

Cuba and the Soviet Union, and reduced internal political space.

In seeking to understand the consequences of U.S. policy, a comparison would be helpful between Grenada where hostile U.S. rhetoric stopped short of destabilization, and Nicaragua where the United States organized and directed an insurgency. By 1983, the New Jewel Movement was entangled in the contradictions of its militarization strategy. Grenadians openly disapproved of the militarization of the country, and the New Jewel Movement could not justify this approach while at the same time trying to boost tourism. In Nicaragua, U.S. hostility facilitated and justified the militarization of the revolution. In brief, U.S. policy is unlikely to have an effect on the direction of the revolution in the short or medium-term, but it can affect the degree of its militance, dependence on the Soviet Union and Cuba, and political polarization.

Still, it must be recognized that Soviet President Mikhail Gorbachev has transformed Soviet foreign policy. Instead of exacerbating regional conflicts in Southern Africa, the Middle East, Southeast Asia, and Central America, he has encouraged his clients and allies to negotiate peaceful solutions. The question is whether his new approach will last and what effect it would have on revolutions in the Caribbean basin. If the competition between the United States and the Soviet Union receded in the Caribbean basin, then the United States ought to be more relaxed about revolutionary turmoil since the probability of a genuine Soviet threat materializing would be sharply reduced. The indirect security perspective is more useful in explaining this new development precisely because the Soviet threat is diminished but not eliminated.

Why should the United States be concerned about a regime's military relationship with the Soviet Union or Cuba? Let us look first at the worst case, the installation of Soviet missiles. One could argue that these present less of a strategic threat to the United States than nuclear missiles fired from Soviet submarines off the coasts of the United States. Indeed, even during the missile crisis in 1962, President John F. Kennedy was less concerned with whether the military balance of power had changed than that the missiles "would have *politically* changed the balance of power; it would have appeared to—and appearances contribute to reality."[18]

Should the United States have risked global annihilation just because the political-psychological balance might have appeared to have shifted? What are the geopolitical consequences of such a shift? Subjective *perceptions* of power have always been important in shaping international relations. The launching of Sputnik led some in the Third World—perhaps even Fidel Castro—to believe that the Soviet Union represented the future, and it also provoked the United States into a "space race." Leaders compete or align their nations based on their perceptions of the balance of power, broadly defined.

If the United States did not respond to the Soviet installation of missiles in Cuba, international perceptions of the balance of power would have changed to favor the Soviet Union, with potentially serious consequences. Each time one superpower uses military force—either directly or indirectly—or expands its military relationships in a region near the other, perceptions of the global balance change. Neither power can ignore such changes, but it is equally dangerous for one superpower to interpret all such changes in the world as threats to its vital interests.

The response should depend on the change. Few in the U.S. government believed that U.S. sanctions would force the Soviet Union to withdraw its troops from Afghanistan, but many thought that if the United States didn't respond at all, then the Soviets might conclude that it could repeat such an exercise with impunity.

There are many U.S. security interests related to the Soviet-Latin American military relationship. In order of declining importance, the United States has interests in preventing the Soviet Union and Cuba from:

1. Establishing military bases or gaining access to naval facilities
2. Stationing troops
3. Delivering sophisticated weapons
4. Maintaining advisors
5. Using the country as a platform to assist or permit cross-border violence

Each affects the balance of perceptions and power in the region, but the appropriate response depends on the significance of the Soviet act and what is effective.

Finally, there is the question of the "demonstration effect." Contrasted with the domino theory, the demonstration effect suggests that if a small government in the Caribbean basin adopts an anti-U.S. posture and the United States fails to respond, that other governments might choose a similar approach for either domestic political or other reasons. This does not constitute a threat to the United States, and a military response of any kind would be counterproductive. Sometimes, no response would be the best; other times, the United States should choose an appropriate and private way to demonstrate that such a posture has a price.

In brief, the United States does have security interests in preventing a hostile, Marxist-Leninist, anti-U.S. group from coming to power by violent means. If such a group does attain power, then the United States has a security interest in limiting its military relationship with the Soviet Union and Cuba and in preventing it from transferring arms to other revolutionaries. But such threats are not direct, and they do not require an unlimited response.

Policies: Escapes and Exits

A statement of these security interests is no guide for policy. While the United States cannot and should not ignore a situation in which these security interests are affected, the response can range widely, from a démarche to military action. Nor should one equate a security interest—a preference—with a security threat. While the United States has an interest in preventing Soviet advisors or troops from being in Nicaragua, their presence does not constitute a threat to the United States.

Let us now address the questions: How should the United States prevent Marxist-Leninist groups from coming to power? If the United States should fail, how should it relate to the revolution in order to prevent the occurrence of worst-case scenarios, e.g., complete dependence on the Soviet Union and support for insurgencies?

In preventing such groups from attaining power, the main challenge and preoccupation of U.S. policymakers is not with the revolutionaries but with the incumbent dictator. The problem is not managing revolutionary change, but rather trying to deal with a political succession where a process does not exist and trust between the contending parties is scarce.[19] Guerrilla struggles in El Salvador and Guatemala testify to the fact that revolutionary turmoil is hardly confined to countries with longstanding dictators. The challenge posed for U.S. policymakers in these countries is not much different than in succession crises, except that history suggests that succession crises are more likely to lead to *successful* revolutions and thus represent a more immediate and difficult problem for the United States.

Because the terrain is a developing country, and the connection between that country's political crisis and U.S. national security is indirect, the task for U.S. policymakers is how to influence political change in a sensitive, developing country. The U.S. can no longer do this effectively by itself as its policies in the Caribbean basin often evoke from local nationalists the opposite of what it seeks. To influence political change, the United States has to reduce and adapt its objectives to the perspectives of other nations in the area. It has to lower its goals and expectations to succeed in achieving any of them.

In its attempt to keep revolutionaries from power, the United States has often made pacts with right-wing dictators, which in turn have worsened problems for the poor and, in the long term, for the United States. If faced with a choice of leftist revolutionaries and rightist dictators, some liberal U.S. citizens advocate supporting the left as they offer the most for the poor, and "history is on their side"; conservatives advocate supporting the right because history has shown that the probability of a democratic evolution has been greater from the right than the left.[20] The United States has never chosen the leftist option and is unlikely ever to do so for reasons noted above. No government wants a neighbor who considers it an enemy, or whose philosophy of governance is inimical to its values. The rightist option looks good to some in retrospect, but it is worth recalling that it has been rejected by administrations as different as Eisenhower, Carter, and, in several cases (notably the Philippines and Haiti), Reagan.

If the revolutionaries take power as they did in Cuba and Nicaragua, policymakers face a different challenge: How to promote U.S. interests toward a regime that views the United States as opposed to its principal goals? In dealing with revolutions, the United States has had few successes. Some U.S. policies have contributed to the outcome that the United States wanted to avoid, while others failed to achieve any objective.

Experience would suggest that a *good* relationship between revolutionaries after they come to power and the United States is unlikely: the issue is not how to achieve a good relationship but, rather, how to avoid a very bad relationship. Certainly, if the United States avoids confronting the regime, and it denies the regime a credible enemy, then a long-term evolution of the regime becomes more likely.

But in the immediate aftermath of the revolution, when the United States has had its most flexible policy, the new regime has been the most rabidly anti-U.S.. As time has passed, U.S. policy has hardened, and the chance that experience might have bred moderation in the revolutionary regime was lost. Unfortunately, the U.S. and the revolutionaries have been out of sequence.

There is both a short-term and a longer-term exit from this self-defeating cycle. In the short-term, the United States needs to define its interests and its capabilities with precision. The United States has a global security interest in limiting the nature of a revolutionary regime's military relationship with the Soviet Union and Cuba; it has a regional security interest in preventing the regime from transferring arms to Marxist guerrillas; and it has a political interest in expanding the future prospects for democracy. As to the first interest, the United States has the credibility as well as the capability to secure that objective. The second and third objectives cannot be attained by unilateral U.S. action, and a militant response—such as a covert war—is more likely than not to push these objectives further away. The only response to these objectives that stands any possibility of success is a collective response among democratic governments in the region.

After a decade of war and instability in Central America, the outlines of what could conceivably become a new collective security arrangement has emerged. The Contadora Initiative of Venezuela, Colombia, Mexico, and Panama defined the parameters of an agreement that acknowledged the special U.S. security interests in containing Soviet military ambitions in the region and in ceasing support for insurgencies. In other words, the initiative addressed the global and regional security interests of the United States. The Reagan administration did not oppose the pursuit of these interests; it resisted the initiative only because it believed that Contadora could not secure those interests and, by leaving the Sandinistas in power, would eventually jeopardize them.

The Central American presidents improved on the Contadora Initiative by addressing the problem of political succession and democracy in the region. Both initiatives accept the collective right of Latin Americans to limit an individual government's external relationships and to influence the way it chooses its leaders. Prior to the 1980s, the principle of nonintervention would have precluded any foreign government from legitimately trying to influence a government's external or internal policies. The conceptual barrier to building a new collective security arrangement has been leaped; whether policymakers can lift their governments over that barrier remains to be seen.

The first step in addressing the longer-term challenge of ending conflict between the United States and revolutionaries is to recognize that responsibility is shared by both sides, and the conflict will end only when *both* change their policies. Of course, suspicions not only prevent that from occurring, but the distrust leads each to interpret the other's behavior in a way that exacerbates the conflict. Both are imprisoned—or, because of exaggerated perceptions, imprismed—in a dilemma from which they cannot extricate themselves.

Each has a self-fulfilling prophecy about the other—the United States suspects the revolutionaries are Marxist-Leninist allies of the Soviet Union, and the revolutionaries suspect that the United States will undermine their revolution.[21] Even if one side tries to suppress its suspicions, as the United States tried to do in Nicaragua and Grenada, the other side will unwittingly provide fresh evidence as to why those suspicions are justified.

Precisely because the self-fulfilling prophecy is *mutual*, one side cannot escape by itself. Trusted intermediaries can help find an exit by convincing the revolutionaries that the United States will support their goals for social justice if they do not ally with the Soviet Union or Cuba. At the same time, the intermediaries—perhaps a group of democratic countries or leaders—would try to convince the United States that the Marxists will not invite the Soviet Union or Cuba if the United States assists them in developing their country. The intermediaries would serve as the guarantors of the agreement and try to prevent suspicions from becoming prophecies. Jimmy Carter and the Council of Freely-Elected Heads of Government played a similar role during the Nicaraguan electoral process—reinforcing positive steps by the Sandinista government and the opposition to insure that the election would be free and fair and respected by both sides.

The United States and Latin American revolutionaries have been imprismed in a past that has served neither's interest. They have believed the worst in the other, and as Cole Blasier put it so well, neither has been disappointed.[22] The question for the future is whether a new collective security arrangement—directed and monitored by independent Latin American countries consulting and possibly collaborating with the United States—can reformulate the relationship so that all sides act to try to bring out the best, not the worst, in the others.[23]

Notes

1. Abraham Lowenthal, *Partners in Conflict: The United States and Latin America* (Baltimore: Johns Hopkins University Press, 1987), p. 64. Lowenthal defines "national insecurity" as "the discomfort of coping with loss of control."
2. Arnold Wolfers, "National Security as an Ambiguous Symbol," in *Discord and Collaboration* (Baltimore: Johns Hopkins University Press, 1962).
3. Walter LaFeber, *Inevitable Revolutions* (New York: W.W. Norton, 1983), p. 15.
4. For a perceptive essay on the nature of revolution, see Chalmers Johnson, *Revolutionary Change*, 2nd ed. (Stanford: Stanford University Press, 1982).
5. Fidel Castro, *Nothing Can Stop the Course of History*, interview by Jeffrey M. Elliot and Mervyn M. Dymally (New York: Pathfinder Press, 1986), p. 7.
6. Maurice Bishop, "We Proudly Share the Noble Dreams of Martin and Malcolm," address to the Sixth Annual Dinner of TransAfrica, Washington, D.C., June 8, 1983, reprinted in *In Nobody's Backyard: Maurice Bishop's Speeches, 1979-83*, Chris Searle, ed. (London: Zed Books, 1984), p. 237.
7. "The Great Challenge," interviews with Jamie Wheelock, May-July 1983, reprinted in *Nicaragua: The Sandinista People's Revolution: Speeches* (New York: Pathfinder Press, 1985), p. 146.
8. Stephen Schlesinger and Stephen Kinzer, *Bitter Fruit: The Untold Story of the American Coup in Guatemala* (New York: Doubleday, 1982), pp. 220-221.
9. For a description and analysis of these trends, see Robert Pastor, *U.S. Foreign Economic Policy: The Dynamics of the Debate* (U.N. Economic Commission for Latin America and the Caribbean, 1986), and *U.S. Foreign Investment and Latin America: The Impact on Employment* (Inter-American Development Bank, 1984).
10. On Mexico, See James W. Wilkie, *The Mexican Revolution: Federal Expenditures and Social Change Since 1910* (Berkeley: University of California Press, 1970), pp. 276-77. On Nicaragua, the Swedish government financed a *Report of an Economic Mission to the Government of Nicaragua*, led by Dr. Lance Taylor 1989, unpublished paper, p. 4. For an account of this report, see Peter Passell, "For Sandinistas, Newest Enemy is Hard Times," *New York Times*, July 6, 1989, p. 6.
11. Robert O. Keohane and Joseph S. Nye, Jr., *Power and Interdependence* (Boston: Little, Brown and Company, 1977), p. 44.
12. Abraham F. Lowenthal, "The United States and Latin America: Ending the Hegemonic Presumption," *Foreign Affairs* (October 1976): 201.
13. For the most complete elaboration of this perspective and a critique of the other perspectives, see Lars Shoultz, *National Security and United States Policy toward Latin America* (Princeton, New Jersey: Princeton University Press, 1987).
14. See also Cole Blasier, "Security: The Extracontinental Dimension," in *The United States and Latin America in the 1980s*, ed. Kevin J. Middlebrook and Carlos Rico (Pittsburgh: University of Pittsburgh Press, 1986), pp. 523-564 Especially see pp. 525 and 537.
15. See Adolfo Aguilar Zinser, "Mexico and the Guatemalan Crisis," in *The*

Future of Central America, ed. Richard Fagen and Olga Pellicer (Stanford, 1983).

16. Michael C. Desch, "Turning the Caribbean Flank: Sea-Lane Vulnerability During a European War," *Survival* XXIX, no. 6 (November-December 1987): 528-551.

17. Cited in Charles McC. Mathias, Jr., "Habitual Hatred—Unsound Policy," *Foreign Affairs* (Summer 1983): 1030.

18. Cited in Aida Donald, *JFK and the New Frontier* (N.Y.: Hill and Wang, 1966), p. 112.

19. For a detailed scenario for how the U.S. should manage such succession crises, see Robert Pastor, *Condemned to Repetition: The U.S. and Nicaragua* (Princeton: Princeton University Press, 1987), Chapter 16.

20. Though this argument seems weak in the aftermath of the political earthquakes in Eastern Europe in the winter of 1989, it had a strong following when it was articulated by Jeane Kirkpatrick in "Dictators and Double Standards," *Commentary* 68 (November 1979): 34-45.

21. For the remainder of this chapter, we shall assume that the self-fulfilling prophecies are not initially true. If they are true, then the prospects for reaching agreement are diminished, but there is still a possibility of reaching coexistence.

22. Cole Blasier, *The Hovering Giant: U.S. Responses to Revolutionary Change in Latin America* (Pittsburgh: University of Pittsburgh Press, 1979).

23. I develop these ideas into a proposal in "Securing A Democratic Hemisphere," *Foreign Policy* 73 (Winter 1988-89).

5

Revolution, the Superpowers, and Latin American Security

Marcial Pérez Chiriboga

When I arrived in Washington in 1979, I had the usual complaint of the Latin American diplomat that U.S. public opinion did not give due importance to Latin America. By the time I finished my term of duty in 1984, I was appalled by the overwhelming, though misdirected, interest in Latin America. From generalized frustration at feeling neglected or being taken for granted by the United States, with sporadic bursts of attention such as the "Good Neighbor Policy," the "Alliance for Progress," and the "New Dialogue," each of which left a feeling of frustration or cynicism, we Latin Americans suddenly found ourselves the center of such attention as to leave us astounded. At the same time, we were bewildered at the absence of a coherent policy that would help us to overcome the basic structural problems our countries faced.

Yet, did the United States finally realize the intrinsic importance of Latin America, or, did U.S. opinion reflect the assumption that "Central America" is "Latin America," and that the Central American crisis engulfed the whole hemisphere? In a 1983 address to Congress, President Reagan stated: "The national security of all the Americas is at stake in Central America. We have a vital interest, a moral duty and a solemn responsibility."[1]

Whether, in fact, the national security of the United States is at stake in Central America is a fascinating subject, but one beyond the scope of this chapter. Rather, my purpose is to analyze whether the security of the "rest of the Americas"—that is, the countries of the Western Hemisphere excluding Canada and the United States—is at stake in Central America. In order to do this, I must first define what national security is for a Latin American country, then attempt to see whether the Central American crisis affected or could affect that security. Finally, I will ask how the reaction of the superpowers to the the crisis might bear on that security.

What Is National Security for Venezuela?

Francisco Orrego Vicuña points out that our contemporary era, as perhaps no other, has been characterized by the search for security by the individual, by the nation, and by the international community. He believes that this is due not only to the growing risk of aggression and violence as a social phenomenon, but also to the uncertainty that is inevitable in a period of radical cultural, scientific, and technological change.[2]

Although every country has a concept of national security, each will have its own agenda and priorities. As Celis Noguera points out, the security of some may well be the insecurity of others.[3] It is thus very difficult to define national security in a manner that is applicable to all modern states. I draw on the ideas of a number of Latin Americans on the subject, but, finally, my outline is the definition of national security for one Latin American country: Venezuela.[4] It will not hold for other Latin American states. However, Venezuela does embody many of the diverse features of the region: it is medium size; it is a part of continental South America but is also an Andean, an Atlantic, and a Caribbean country; it has resources but also suffers the economic dislocations of the region.

National security can be viewed either narrowly and strictly defensively or politically and more broadly. Though the distinction may not be absolutely clearcut, it is useful to adapt it for my purposes.[5] For instance, the broader view of Venezuelan national security goals is implied in the message to congress submitting the organic Law of Security and Defense, which defines the security of the nation "as the degree of guarantees which through political, economic, social, or military action, a State can bring to the Nation in order to achieve and safeguard its national objectives."[6]

Security is not limited to "viewing international relations . . . as grounds of threats and perils that must be contained; but also and fundamentally as an ensemble of opportunities for a positive action which promotes solidarity, stimulates agreement on common interests and reduces, through diplomacy, negotiation and compromise the areas of tension and conflict."[7]

Thus, national security would have to include:

1. Preserving territorial integrity. The question of borders is especially important and can become a highly sensitive issue.

In 1972 and 1973, Venezuela held conversations with Colombia on the delimitation of the maritime borders between the two countries. Venezuelan public opinion was intensely interested in this problem; it was not only media coverage but a deep-felt concern in all walks of Venezuelan life. Taking up a post in the Hague a year later, I had a chance to see the Dutch public reaction to the judgment of the International Court of Justice in the North Sea Continental Shelf Cases (Federal Republic of Germany/Denmark; Federal

Republic of Germany/Netherlands). The average person had no idea what it was about; and what you could call qualified opinion felt that while it was too bad that the case was lost, after all was it really that vital? If this had happened in Venezuela, there would have been a major crisis.

It is not that Europeans are not patriotic or are not willing to defend their territorial integrity. History and the graveyards of European wars (especially the Great War) give categorical evidence to the contrary. But the Europeans have seen so many modifications of their borders that they can view these questions with a different perspective. An Alsatian born at the turn of the century has seen his territory change hands four times.

2. Safeguarding the population against acts that endanger the physical welfare of the people. Protection from violence of any sort is an essential element of national security.

3. Ensuring the commerce that is essential for the development—or even the economic existence—of the country. Venezuela depends on its oil exports as the mainstay of its economic life. If passage on the sealanes were interrupted, national security would certainly be affected. Likewise Venezuela depends, to a degree that worries many Venezuelans, on imports of many manufactured, semimanufactured and agricultural products. It needs to import a considerable amount of the food necessary to feed its people.

4. Avoiding disorderly influxes of people. Venezuela is a country of immigration and in the last quarter century has become a country of asylum. We are proud of that. But any upheaval in neighboring countries that would cause a wave of refugees would affect our national security. Thus, Venezuela is susceptible to the "feet people" issue.

5. Ensuring the maintenance of the democratic system of government that the Venezuelan people have given themselves. It can be debated whether a particular system of government should be equated with the national security of a state. But I consider it indispensable to do so, for it certainly would modify the basic way of life of a nation if a democratic system, respectful of the laws and of human rights, were replaced by a totalitarian or authoritarian regime, be it of the "left" or of the "right."

6. Sustaining the right to develop its own foreign policy. In blunt words, a state should be able to choose its friends and decide who are its enemies according to its interpretation of its national interest.

7. Promoting a friendly, or at least a nonhostile, environment. Does this mean that the security of a state is affected by the form of government of its neighbors? This point is critical to this chapter. The preamble of the Venezuelan Constitution establishes a mandate to promote democracy:

> Uphold the democratic order as the only and unrenounceable way of assuring the rights and dignity of its citizens, and favor its pacific extension to all the Peoples of the Earth.[8]

Was the intention of the drafters of the constitution a purely altruistic one or one based on a belief that if democracy were established in other, and especially neighboring countries, it would help consolidate democracy in Venezuela? No doubt it was a combination of both. If one reads the history of Venezuela and remembers the political situation in the region when the constitution was adopted (1961), the second reason was certainly in the minds of the legislators.

This list of the elements of national security is not very different, I suspect, from similar lists for most countries. It does, however, extend beyond Orrego Vicuña's purely defensive and reactive definition in two ways. It describes the state's environment as a rather broad geographic zone. And it has an ideological content in its commitment to democracy. Unlike a list written for a superpower, however, or perhaps for Cuba because of its commitment to revolutionary internationalism, Venezuela's zone is regional, not global.

If Venezuela's definition of national security is not all that different from that of other countries, great and small, the question becomes how to make it operational. How is it applied to specific situations? With particular regard to Central America, how should Venezuela deal with the rise of a revolutionary regime in its vital zone?

Is a Revolutionary Regime In Central America a Security Threat?

There is a good deal of confusion over what is a "revolutionary regime." Is it the product of a process that overthrows a tyranny in order to change the political, social and economic structures? Is "revolutionary" synonymous with a Marxist-Leninist regime, or with "socialism"? For Venezuela:

1. An "indigenous revolution" would not be a security threat.
2. A regime with Marxist participation would not per se be a security threat.
3. A Marxist-Leninist regime would not necessarily be a security threat.
4. It would be the foreign policies of those regimes, if aggressive, that could be security threats.

If "revolutionary regimes" were defined more loosely, the possibility of "peaceful coexistence" or of "ideological plurality" would be clear. The presidents of Venezuela and Peru make a strong reference to this point in the joint declaration signed in 1973, when they: "Affirm their respect for ideological pluralism in Latin America and to the maintenance of relations between countries with different sociopolitical systems; their rejection of any actions destined to isolate any Latin American country for the sole cause of the political orientation of its government."[9]

However, the policies of a Marxist-Leninist government could be a threat to the national security of Latin American countries. Does this statement merely repeat a cliché or is it a fact in international life? The answer depends on three factors: the proximity of the threat, the actual policy of intervention or aggression, and finally the capability for intervention.

The Proximity of the Threat

Evidently, a policy of "exporting the revolution" by Nicaragua would be a menace to Costa Rica, for example, but would it be a danger to Argentina or to Venezuela? This raises questions about the breadth of a state's vital zones and about "domino effects." Viron Vaky points out that:

> [U.S.] administration officials have repeatedly affirmed that, unless contained, Marxism-Leninism (read Soviet/Cuban power) will move inexorably south into South America and North to Mexico, eventually threatening the United States itself.
>
> The flaw in the domino argument is that it is presented as if it functioned automatically. What happens in one country obviously influences what happens in another, but how much and in what form, and with what results depends upon circumstances. The process is not automatic, especially with regard to countries with very different histories, conditions, strengths and weaknesses. The "ripple effect" within the confines of the relatively similar nations of Central America is one thing; its extension to Mexico, Colombia, Venezuela and the United States is something else.[10]

I tend to agree. Still, how far does the ripple go, or when do the dominoes stop falling?

Certainly an upheaval in a bordering country is a cause for grave concern. The answers to the questions, "Where will it stop?" and "When am I endangered?," bring up the issue of what are "the vital zones" to a given country. The answer is critical but may change with the times. For instance, has the rhetoric that Central America is vital to the United States convinced world opinion or the American public? If Central America is vital, why has it been so neglected?

Presenting too rigid a definition of "vital zones" is dangerous intellectually and politically, for it would seem to indicate that a state is "drawing the line." If a great or an emerging power repeatedly does so, it can cause concern to its weaker neighbors. Nevertheless, a country should have clear ideas, and policy priorities, about which countries are more important from a national security point of view.

For Venezuela, a rough delineation of a vital zone would extend through Central America to the south of Mexico, north through the Antilles, east to Grenada and Trinidad and Tobago, and south to Brazil north of the Amazon, including the Guianas.[11] Venezuela cannot be indifferent to what happens in this zone.

The Actual Policy of a Marxist-Leninist Government

The existence per se of a Marxist-Leninist regime is not necessarily a national security threat, but it may begin with an ingrained hostility to other sorts of regimes. One author states: "According to the National Directorate, a region as small as Central America allowed for only one of two options: a revolutionary solution for the entire region, given the 'ripple effect' of the Sandinista Revolution, or the eventual defeat of Nicaragua."[12] Sandinista leader Tomás Borge has been quoted as saying in Pyonyang: "the Nicaraguan revolution will not be content until the imperialists have been overthrown in all parts of the world."[13]

When that hostility should be regarded as "aggression" is a debated subject. I describe, somewhat arbitrarily, the threats to national security from the policies of a Marxist-Leninist government in three categories:

1. Direct political action, such as wide-scale propaganda, the training of political cadres in destabilization tactics, and the financing of political movements committed to subversion.

2. Indirect military action such as the training of guerrillas, arms shipments, and equipping terrorists. This point raises the issue of whether an increase in the military forces of the Marxist-Leninist government is itself a security menace. When is an armament defensive or offensive? What is an "undue" military buildup? These are subjects on which paranoia feasts, and misinformation and disinformation are common. The safest guideline is the following: until there is a trustworthy system of collective security by and for Latin American nations, a massive increase in the military potential of a country in the area can lead to an arms race by other countries. It is thus destabilizing, if not directly threatening.

3. Direct military action. Naval blockade, air raids, invasion, and establishing guerrilla *focos*.

The Short-Term Capacity and Long-Term Nature of "Revolutionary" Regimes

Governments that hold threatening policies may not have the capacity to carry them out. If they do not, then the attitude of their allies, especially if the ally is a superpower, becomes crucial. However, even if a threatening government can be constrained in the short run, there remains the vexing question, one closely related to the nature of revolutions, whether it is an inexorable desideratum for a Marxist-Leninist government to foster revolutions in other countries. If so, any "bargain" with it may be broken whenever the revolutionary regime feels it has the capacity to do so.

In the instance of Nicaragua, it has been argued that the state would be willing to renounce intervention in other countries if their own internal system were not imperiled by outside forces. For them, a deal might be more than tactical. They would agree to a trade-off:

> Managua's support for the Salvadorian revolutionaries would cease in exchange for the termination of Washington's support for the counterrevolutionaries on the Honduras border. Further, Nicaragua should not be asked to make concessions at home of a strategic nature. This option of a Pax Finlandia would [have been] acceptable to some in the Reagan administration. It would [have been] equally attractive to the more dogmatic among the members of the National Directorate for it would permit their move to an orthodox domestic socialist model.[14]

U. S. Assistant Secretary for Inter-American Affairs, Thomas Enders, apparently offered such a Pax Finlandia in 1981, and that idea emerged clearly in López Portillo's proposition of February 1982.

Was a Pax Finlandia possible? Would it have required a "Nicaraguan Tito?" It is said that all comparisons are unwise, and historical comparisons are especially dangerous. Yet to judge the possibility of any negotiated agreement it was necessary to know whether the leaders of the revolution were "Stalinists" or "Trotskyites": did they believe in consolidating socialism in their state as the foremost priority to which other goals must be sacrificed; or did they believe in the "permanent revolution," not only as an ideological obligation but as the only way of consolidating their regime?

With respect to Nicaragua, the question was hard to answer. But it must be asked, not only in the case of that country, but in case other "revolutionary" movements take power.

The other side of the coin is whether the United States would accept the consolidation of a Marxist-Leninist regime in Central America and the Caribbean if it were guaranteed that it would contain its revolution within its borders. The Reagan administration seemed to have been so prepared in 1981. And the report of the Kissinger Commission answered in the affirmative with respect to Cuba:

> Should Havana, for whatever reason, change its basic attitude and be prepared for genuine coexistence with the United States, we, in turn, should be prepared to negotiate seriously. Such coexistence would have to involve an end to Cuban support for insurgency in Central America and promotion

of revolutions elsewhere in the world. We, in turn, should then be prepared
to live with Cuba and lift existing restrictions.[15]

The Kissinger Commission was categorical about coexisting with an
established and consolidated regime. But would the United States accept a
trade-off that consolidated another Marxist regime in the hemisphere? The
question remains open.

Superpower Reactions: A Security Threat?

For a Latin American, the drama of Central America did not start in 1979, or
even in 1959. It has been with us all of our lives. The situation was not
invented by Cuba. In 1932, in El Salvador between 10,000 and 30,000 people
were massacred in a brief period of time, but no television brought it live and
in color to U.S. and European homes. The oppression, the hunger, the
injustice have always been there.

So, too, U.S. intervention has always been there. I noted the paradox: if
the area was vital to the United States, why was it always neglected? The
neglect was with respect to helping the people overcome their fundamental
economic and social problems. But neglect did not mean there was no
intervention. "Since 1823, the United States has conducted more than 70
military operations in Central America and the Caribbean without a
declaration of war."[16] The number may not be exact, but the impression of
constant interventions, almost always on behalf of the wrong causes and of
the wrong people, is clearly engraved in our minds.

For the Soviet Union's part, it has acted with masterful opportunism in
the area. It did not cause the Cuban revolution nor the Sandinista victory. The
Sandinistas were actively supported by Costa Rica, Mexico, Panama, and
Venezuela, as well as by Cuba. "While governments like the Venezuelan of
CAP or the Panamanian could display an active solidarity—and how
active!—with the Sandinistas, the Cuban government acted with such
prudence and caution that it could be confused with inhibition."[17]

Not one Soviet life was lost in these events, while the Soviet Union
acquired an invaluable base and ally in Cuba and was in a "no lose" situation
in Central America. In the context of the Soviet Union's expansionary
policies of the pre-Gorbachev era, if the Sandinistas had consolidated their
power and had a Marxist-Leninist regime, it would have been in the Soviet
interest. If the "domino theory" had become reality, it would have been to
their benefit. If the United States intervened militarily, the Soviet Union
could have shrugged it off as part of the realities of geographic fatalism and
at the same time could have obtained tremendous political advantages from
the anti-American reaction in the area. It would have been a propaganda

bonus for them. In the era of Gorbachev, the defeat of the Sandinistas in the 1990 election was also to the Soviet Union's benefit: It provides the Soviet Union with a perfect excuse to cut down on its assistance to Nicaragua, which serves the new Soviet policy of retrenchment in overseas commitments very well.

The Soviet-Cuban presence in the area has become a fact of life. Both that presence and U.S. concern about it has given a new and different dimension to the crisis. If the problems of Central America and the Caribbean are conceived in a strictly East-West perspective, a security problem for the Latin American countries is all the greater. Barring all out nuclear war—in which case all security considerations would be irrelevant—many dangers could occur. One example is interdiction or harassment of sealanes. In the case of Venezuela, for instance, after February 1942 German submarines began to attack Venezuelan oil tankers in the Caribbean with the result that oil revenues fell of by one-third in that year.[18] This is hypothetical; it is unlikely that it would happen without further and more far-reaching consequences. Nevertheless, before 1979, was it imaginable that ships in the Persian Gulf would be attacked over a period of several years?

More dramatically still, the possibilities of a regional war seemed real. The governments of Venezuela and Mexico felt that Central America was on the verge of war in October 1982. So did many others in 1986. "The spreading effects of 'proxy' strategies have led to increasing turmoils and growing polarization and to what one observer has called 'the second Spanish Civil War.'"[19] Would these wars be limited or would they spread?

Above all what would be the policy of the superpowers? The Kissinger Commission says:

> A great power can choose what challenges to respond to, but it cannot choose where those challenges come—or when. Nor can it avoid the necessity of deliberate choice. Once challenged, a decision not to respond to it is fully as consequential as a decision to respond. We are challenged now in Central America. No agony of indecision will make that challenge go away. No wishing it were easier will make it easier.[20]

Final Comments: Contadora

My aim has been to reach some conclusions about what national security is to a Latin American country; whether that security is affected by the installation of a "revolutionary regime" in Central America or by the policy of that regime and if that regime can implement that policy on its own or must it be a surrogate of the Soviet Union. Finally, I attempted to analyze the reaction of the superpowers to the Central American crisis and the effect of that reaction on Latin America's security.

The Contadora process reflected my conclusions. It was extremely important as a Latin American initiative. Its very existence was positive. Even if it was not totally successful, it was a watershed because it represented Latin Americans trying to find a Latin American solution to a Central American problem. One could almost say that in the case of Contadora the means justified the ends.

The four countries that form the Contadora Group were genuinely concerned with the dangers of war in Central America. For the Venezuelan Government, that certainly was the case. The advent of the "support group," consisting of Argentina, Brazil, Peru, and Uruguay, showed the concern of these countries for the problem. Did they feel their security was affected? Evidently so, at least to some degree. They acted to forestall a wider conflict that might spill unpredictably out of Central America.

Finally, the Kissinger Commission was right when it stated:

> A modernization of the regional security system is imperative, just as there can be no real security without economic growth and social justice, so there can be no prosperity without security.[21]

It was also right in recognizing the linkage between democratization and security in the region. There will never be stability without the indispensable economic and social reforms carried out by democratic governments respectful of human rights and accountable to the people. Until this happens, there will be revolutionary processes.

Can they be prevented simply by the use of force or the threat of the use of force? Lefeber's story is very pertinent:

> In 1906 senior military officials asked President Theodore Roosevelt for a special favor. They wondered whether he might give U.S. diplomats and naval commanders on the spot sufficient authority to stop Central American revolts and permanently stabilize the area. The request reached the desk of Assistant Secretary of State Alvey A. Adee. A wise, experienced man, Adee had served as the department's permanent bureaucracy for a quarter century. "How could we do this" he jotted on the request, "without actually acquiring all these little countries?" The proposal promptly died.[22]

Must we always fear revolutionary processes? The Kissinger Committee eloquently presents the case: "If the insurgents were in fact the vehicles for democratic and social progress, the entire security issue would be moot. They would no longer be the problem, but rather the solution."[23]

Notes

1. Quoted in Viron Vaky, "Reagan's Central American Policy: An Isthmus Restored," in *Central America: Anatomy of Conflict,* ed. Robert S. Leiken (New York: Pergamon Press, 1984), p. 237.

2. Francisco Orrego Vicuña, "Libertad y seguridad nacional," in *Defensa nacional, seguridad interna y bien común,* ed. Genaro Arriagada et al. (Maracaibo: Irfes, 1977), p. 123.

3. Carlos E. Celis Noguera, "La seguridad y su estrategia" in *Seguridad y defensa,* ed. Elio J. Orta Zambrano et al. (Caracas: Presidencia de la República, Consejo Nacional de Seguridad y Defends, Secretaría Permanente, 1981), p. 27.

4. In addition to Celis Noguera and Orrego Vicuña, some of the most important of those writers are: Julio S. Corredor Ruiz, *La planificación estratégica* (Caracas: Oficina Central de Información, 1985); Teodoro Petkoff, "Venezuela en el mundo, seguridad nacional desde la perspectiva del cambio social" in *Seguridad, defensa y democracia en Venezuela,* ed. Anibal Romero (Caracas: Equinocco, 1980); Quoted in Carlos Celis Noguera, *Casos estratégicos de actualidad* (Caracas: Rizo, 1981), p. 18; Quoted in Arriagada et al., *Defensa Nacional,* p. 90; Quoted in Roberto Calvo, "Doctrin de la seguridad nacional" in *Iglesia y seguridad nacional,* ed. Equipo Seladoc (Salamanca: Sigueme, 1980), p. 23; Arístides Calvani, "Seguridad defensa y valores de la persona" in *Seguridad y defensa,* ed. Romero, p. 78; José Manuel Santos, "La seguridad nacional, condición del bien común," in *Defensa nacional,* ed. Arriagada et al., p. 115.

5. Orrego Vicuña, "Libertad y seguridad," p. 125

6. Quoted in Carlos Celis Noguera, "Seguridad defensa y participación" in *Seguridad, defensa,* ed. Romero, p. 86.

7. Aníbal Romero, "Pensamiento geopolítico, seguridad y democracia" in *Seguridad, defensa* ed. Romero, p. 65.

8. *Constitución de la República de Venezuela* (Caracas: Secretaría del Sendao de la Republica, 1968), p. 2.

9. Rafael Caldera, *La solidaridad pluralista de America Latina* (Caracas: Officina Central de Información, 1973), p. 268.

10. Vaky, "Isthmus Restored," p. 239.

11. Here I agree with Rodríguez Iturbe, who says:

In the west all of Colombia, through Panama and Central America (Costa Rica, Nicaragua, El Salvador, Honduras, Belize and Guatemala) including the south-eastern states of Mexico (Yucatan, Campeche, Quinana Roo, Tabasco and Chiapas). In the East, the rosary of islands of the Eastern Caribbean, the windward islands, from the Virgin Islands to Grenada and Trinidad-Tobago. The vital zone is complemented by the part of Brazil north of the Amazon, from the Leticia Triangle to its outlet in the Atlantic (that is, the Northern part of State of Amazonas, the northern part of the State of Para and the territories of Roraima and Ampapa); Suriname, French Guiana and the Republic of Guyana.

Nothing that occurs in that vital zone is indifferent or neutral to the national interest. Any phenomenon in it can be valued as negative or positive for security and defense. And in situations of crisis any positive phenomenon must be supported and potentiated by our external action while any negative phenomenon must be opposed and defeated or at least reduced to its minimum incidence.

Quoted in Aníbal Romero, "Situación Estratégica de Venezuela," *Política Internacional*, no. 1 (eneromayo 1986): 11.

12. Arturo Cruz Sequeira, "The Origins of Sandinista Foreign Policy" in *Central America*, ed. Leiken, p. 104.

13. Quoted in Jeane J. Kirkpatrick, "U.S. Security and Latin America" in *Rift and Revolution*, ed. Howard Wiarda, pp. 18-19.

14. Cruz Sequeira, "Sandinista Foreign Policy," p. 107.

15. *Report of the President's National Bipartisan Commission on Central America* (New York: Macmillan, 1984), pp. 144-145.

16. Victor Millán, "Controlling Conflict in the Caribbean Basin: National Approaches" in *Controlling Latin American Conflicts*, ed. Michael Morris and Victor Millán (Boulder: Westview Press, 1983), pp. 41-42.

17. Petkoff, "Venezuela en el Mundo," p. 128.

18. Sheldon B. Liss, *Diplomacy and Dependency: Venezuela, the United States and the Americas* (Salisbury: Documentary Publications, 1978), p. 117.

19. Vaky, "Isthmus Restored," p. 234.

20. Report of President's Commission, p. 2.

21. Ibid., p. 137.

22. Walter LaFeber, "The Burdens of the Past" in *Central America*, ed. Leiken.

23. Report of President's Commission, p. 105.

6

The Contadora Experience and the Future of Collective Security

Carlos Rico F.

Collective security in the Americas had its heyday during the quarter century after World War II. At that time relations between the United States and Latin America constituted an almost "ideal type" of hegemonic system[1] —the United States had the ability not only to set the basic parameters of "permissible" behavior but also to provide its Latin American neighbors with a good measure of leadership. The fundamental realities underlying this system reflected the general imbalances existing in the political and economic milieu worldwide. However, as those imbalances were modified over the years leading into the 1970s, the hegemonic system underwent significant changes. What slowly emerged was a set of "new realities," summed up by Latin American political observers and actors with such phrases as multipolarity, the "internationalization of domestic politics" (i.e., the renewed presence of European political forces in the region), and "ideological pluralism" (the Latin American version of détente).

One of the most prominent features of this new set of realities was that it provided new alternatives for the Latin American governments (and nongovernmental actors) as they tried to "break out" of the hemisphere in both economic and political terms.[2] The fact that the most sought after of those alternatives, Western Europe and Japan, remained squarely in the Western camp, however, also had an impact at the level of security perceptions. It became increasingly apparent that there was a need to distinguish between common (Western) security concerns and national ones; that not all that was in the national interest of any one ally (even the hegemonic power) was necessarily also in favor of the common good. And since the perception of common concerns and interests is the basis of any truly collective security arrangement, the earlier easy identification of U.S. and common security concerns was bound to be modified. This basic distinction between the defense of *common* interests and the pursuit of basically *national* objectives constitutes the organizing principle of this chapter.[3]

The Contadora Process as a Case Study

The form inter-American collective security might take in the future might well be glimpsed by looking at the Contadora negotiations in Central America during the 1980s. The reason for this is twofold. First, Central America is fertile terrain for analyzing the "new realities." Since the turn of the century the subregion has been externally influenced most heavily by the United States. During the last decade, however, it has become an area of conflict of a particularly intense international dimension. From Israel and the PLO to Cuba and the Soviet Union, including a whole series of middle-range powers, a number of international actors have participated in the evolution of the Central American conflict. As a result, an area that could have been characterized during the postwar years as a zone of U.S. hyperhegemony,[4] where a limited commitment of resources was usually enough for the U.S. government to "correct" apparent deviations from the rules of the game,[5] became in the 1980s an area of intense conflict, where the superpower was unable (at least, until the end of the decade) to dictate its own preferred solution. This evolution of U.S. influence points to important changes that must be taken into account when evaluating one of the more sensitive aspects of inter-American relations: security issues.

Secondly, there is the particular nature of the Contadora process itself. Although relatively new participants in the Central American scene, the four Latin American countries of Colombia, Mexico, Panama, and Venezuela (collectively dubbed Contadora after the Panamanian island from which they launched their effort), came to establish the basic point of reference for most other international actors interested in solving the crisis through negotiations and other peaceful means. Furthermore, they did so despite the fact that the U.S. government was pursuing a quite different set of policies. Because it presented an option to U.S. proposals, the Contadora experience is particularly attractive as a case study of the present state of inter-American relations in the security realm.

In mid-1985 a "support group" consisting of Argentina, Brazil, Peru, and Uruguay (collectively known as the Lima group in reference to the city where their efforts were first announced) transformed the Contadora initiative into one of the few areas in which significant consensus was achieved among key Latin American governments in the security sphere. The fact that the populations of the Contadora countries and the "support group" represented well over 90 percent of the region's total gave them a valid claim to represent the interests of Latin America as a whole.

In utilizing the Contadora negotiations as a case study, this chapter has been divided into four main parts. The first presents the basic cast of characters, identifying their key interests regarding the Central American crisis, particularly security issues. The second compares the policies advanced by the Reagan administration and by the Contadora countries. The third focuses on the main changes in perceptions of the United States and the Contadora group as mediation moved forward. The conclusion speculates on the implications of all this for the future prospects of collective security in the Western Hemisphere.

The Cast of Characters: Basic Interests and Motivations

The Reagan Administration and the Contadora Initiative

The Reagan administration, as did almost all other governments in the world, formally expressed its "support" for Contadora. Its behavior, however, spoke otherwise. Not only did the administration not help the process, but it in fact made matters more difficult at critical junctures. At those moments during the process when the Contadora governments made concrete requests of their North American counterpart that they considered would be helpful to their efforts (as was the case in their visit to the Secretary of State in early 1986, when the need to stop aid to the Nicaraguan contras was raised), those requests were summarily denied The justification given was that to do so would hurt the process instead of helping it! For many political commentators in Latin America two possible sets of arguments explained U.S. behavior.

The first set of alternatives focused on whether the U.S. government was actually or at least potentially interested in a negotiated solution to the crisis. There were two possible answers: (1) the U.S. government supported the possibility of a negotiated solution but was convinced that "big brother knows best" how to increase the possibilities for such an outcome *or* (2) its formal "support" for Contadora was no more than public diplomacy and empty rhetoric, masking a very real, and on occasion quite active, opposition to the process.

If the second alternative was the answer—that is, the United States was opposed to a negotiated solution, its rhetoric notwithstanding—then one was faced with a second set of interesting alternative explanations. These centered on whether U.S. policies were predicated on the notions of defending not only U.S. national interests, but also the interests of the West (which presumably included those Latin American countries committed to the Contadora process). If the U.S. government was in fact trying to protect perceived common interests by *not negotiating,* this would also clearly involve a "big brother knows best" component, only in this case considerably more extreme. The governments of Contadora would be seen as being incapable of understanding their own real security interests and the steps needed to adequately defend them. This was the dominant perception in the initial stages of the Contadora process.

A second alternative was that U.S. behavior in Central America was not directed at defending common interests, but rather at promoting its own perceived *national* interests. In that case, U.S. behavior would seem to indicate a distrust not so much of the abilities and capabilities of the Contadora countries, but their intentions.

Latin American Interests and Motivations

The eight non-Central American governments involved in the Contadora process had some shared interests with the United States. The members of both the Contadora and the Lima groups were not only capitalist countries, but included some of the most constant international allies of the United States. There are well-known differences in the degree to which the governments of these countries have "followed the leader" at crucial moments, but none of them could be identified as an opponent of U.S. interests or, more particularly, as a member of the other superpower's entourage.

The countries also shared some common national interests among themselves. Most of the countries involved could be seen as clear Latin American examples of "middle" or "emerging" powers, which have a general tendency to rely on formal norms and the rule of international law. In fact, the Contadora members included some of the Latin American countries that have played key roles in developing "American international law," in particular the principle of nonintervention A more recent common characteristic of the eight countries is that they were in dire financial straits, and looked to the U.S. government to help them solve their predicaments. That they were willing and able to maintain a Central American policy that put them at odds with the Reagan administration is in that case remarkable.

There were, of course, significant differences among them. Some of the governments within the "Group of Eight" (the four Contadora countries, plus the four "support group" countries) were more favorable to the Sandinista revolution, and even to the revolutionary movement in El Salvador, than were others; but even those governments were quite clear in stating that their sympathies resulted from an understanding that those forces represented legitimate domestic claims and aspirations in their countries, not the interests of the other superpower.

There were also differences of national interests within each group—Contadora and Lima—and between the two groups themselves.

The Original Members of the Contadora Group

From the start there were some significant disagreements among the Contadora countries. Before the launching of the group in early 1983 some of the members, in particular Mexico and Venezuela, had put forth their own proposals vis-à-vis the Central American crisis. It was clear that embarking

on a more multilateral route implied introducing significant changes in each country's previous policies. For some of them this meant expanding their commitments; for others, restricting them. That their original policies were in some cases significantly different makes it all the more remarkable that common ground for the Contadora's proposals was found, and highlights the importance of those points with which they were in agreement.

What, then, were those basic coincidences that kept Contadora together? The kind of exercise represented by Contadora had its most direct antecedent in the role that the same group of countries (minus Panama, plus Costa Rica and Jamaica) played in the negotiations of the Panama Canal treaties. The most interesting similarity was that, in both cases, the possibility of a violent explosion in the area seemed to be present, even if the threat seemed considerably more remote in the case of Panama. In both cases, those states whose own security was threatened by such an explosion mobilized to try to defuse that possibility.

The threat of heightened conflict also helped keep the process going as long as it did. Colombia, Mexico, Panama and Venezuela were the "frontline states" in the Central American crisis. After the Central Americans, it was they who would have suffered the most immediate consequences if regional conflict could not have been contained. They did not believe that a "military solution" could be a "surgical" strike like the Grenada operation. Rather, they felt it would lead to a wider conflict. A wider conflict could not be expected to be of a short duration. The proven resilience of the Salvadoran revolutionary movement and the considerable defense capabilities of the Sandinista revolution made that clear.

Geography, while serving as a basis for common interests, also accounted for some of the difficulties encountered in the Contadora mediation attempt. That the United States was a part of the same geopolitical neighborhood constrained the Contadora's ability to play a major role in looking for alternative solutions. It is not easy to be a "regional influential" in the same immediate region as a superpower, which has fewer incentives to "delegate" in that region than it may have in other areas. What some might consider overreaction on the part of the U.S. government could also be related to its being in the immediate vicinity of Central America.

The Lima "Support Group"

The South American countries of the Lima support group did not face the same kind of geopolitical imperative as the Contadora group. For the latter, the eruption of a wider conflict in Central America was of concern regardless of internal politics—it was a truly national interest. For the support group the question of military confrontations in Central America played a smaller role both in it's foreign policy agendas and in their domestic political debates. In

the case of the support group members, their interests in the problem stemmed more from governmental policy than national interest. Changing governments brought changing policies toward the Central American crisis. This is illustrated in the example of Argentina. The previous Argentinian government stood squarely on the side of the Reagan administration in the Central American crisis. However, the Alfonsin foreign policy team showed great interest in the Contadora process from its first moments in office and later became a crucial piece in the creation of the support group.

What were the policies that were dependent on regime change and not permanent national imperatives? A common feature among the four Lima actors was that all were "new democracies," with Peru in the role of the young old lady. Their role in restoring institutional legality to their own countries increased the relevance of the "rule of law" to their own domestic politics. It would be quite difficult for them to openly support a U.S. policy in Central America that was widely perceived in the region to involve clear and open violations of law and principle.

However, while this may help to explain why the Lima group countries did not support U.S. policy, it does not sufficiently account for their decision to join the Contadora process. A key element may have been that they agreed with the Contadora countries that a military "solution" must be avoided. The reasons for this seem to go beyond the defense of the rule of law, and lie in the political situations in which these countries found themselves at the time. The domestic problems and the political coalitions supporting their regimes were such that they could ill afford an intensification of domestic pressures from outbursts of anti-U.S. feelings, feelings that might result from more open direct military participation in the Central American conflict by the United States.

Thus, the motives of Argentina, Brazil, Peru, and Uruguay were less urgent and immediate than those of the original members of the Contadora group. The Lima group did not have necessary incentives to play a leading role in launching the initiative, but its motivations became increasingly important as time progressed.

Initial Diagnoses and Policy Prescriptions

From the viewpoint of the Contadora countries, U.S. policies seemed not only dangerous, but unnecessary. At first, U.S. proposals were thought to flow from a fundamentally flawed diagnosis of the origins of the Central American crisis. Perhaps taking too seriously the public statements that dominated the Reagan administration's first two years, Contadora seemed to assume that the U.S. government actually believed the crisis was the result of Soviet activities undertaken through its Cuban "proxies." The perceived

emphasis on the military aspects of the conflict was thought to flow from the U.S. government's perhaps mistaken—but real—perception of a security threat.

Perceptions of U.S. Perceptions and Policy Prescriptions

The basic arguments that U.S. policymakers were seen to be developing were actually quite simple. Their assumption was that external subversion was a key determinant of the crisis, and the challenge to be met was fundamentally military in nature. There was no lack of public statements to this effect. One of the clearest and most articulate was put forward by Jeane Kirkpatrick in her indictment of U.S. policy toward the region under the Carter administration. Analyzing the fall of the Nicaraguan regime in 1979, Kirpatrick presented as a crucial component of its demise a set of misguided policies on the part of a U.S. government that never understood that "the Somoza regime had never rested on popular will (but instead on manipulation, force and habit), and *was not being ousted by it. It was instead succumbing to arms and soldiers.*"[6]

In Latin America this line of reasoning was perceived to have a very simple bottom line. In Nicaragua, for example, the perception was that the Reagan administration saw the problem as "not Somoza," but "Cuban arms." Given this diagnosis, it was not surprising that the U.S. government would emphasize military options to deal with insurgent forces (or governments erected by them) that after all were not seen as embodiments of understandable and legitimate domestic demands, but as "fifth columns" of the Soviet Union. However, it is essential to realize that for the U.S. policymakers, the central point was not the nature or source of instability in the area. The issue was the *consequences* of such instability, which were perceived as constituting a security threat. The most basic of those *consequences* was thought to be the strengthening of the U.S. global adversary: the Soviet Union. Indeed, even after the "1984 Kissinger report on Central America"[7] shed light on the domestic sources of unrest, the basic U.S. policy prescriptions remained unchanged.

Among the disagreements between the U.S. government and its Latin American counterparts were questions concerning the only *government* established in the region as a result of a crisis in the previous political structures—the Sandinista regime. This was to be expected because a government was seen as having the most compelling claim to the protection of international law, and it did not seem as if these claims were being duly honored by certain U.S. policies. The issue was particularly important in the first stages of the Contadora initiative; problems associated with the Salvadoran insurgency clearly took a backseat.

The Contadora governments found this particular U.S. argument worrisome. Emphasis was being put on external sources of instability, closely tying the Nicaraguan process to "Soviet-Cuban" actions. Once the revolutionary forces in El Salvador erupted, the same emphasis made it almost unavoidable that, in the discourse (and the minds?) of U.S. policymakers, a new link was added to the Soviet "chain of command"; instability in El Salvador was to be understood as having one of its basic sources in "Soviet-Cuban-*Nicaraguan*" actions.

The implications of this logic for the Sandinista regime were not hard to see. Nicaragua was perceived as already "lost," as already a part of the Soviet camp. Thus, the only solution for the situation was to overthrow the revolutionary government. After all, one does not negotiate with enemies if one can defeat them. Negotiations can only proceed as a result of either the perceived existence of common interests or the need on the part of the actors involved to take "second best" options. The way in which the U.S. mindset was perceived left little room for either of those possibilities.

Contadora's Alternative Proposals

The Contadora countries saw this U.S. argument as fundamentally flawed, not because of its internal logic (which could be seen as quite compelling), but because it was built on erroneous premises. They presented an alternative diagnosis of the crisis that provided the basis for a different set of policy proposals.

They put emphasis on the *domestic,* rather than external, sources of the Central American crisis. Problems were seen as emerging from the economic, social, and political realities of the Central American countries themselves. There were international factors that contributed to the conflict, but the most important among them were not associated with foreign subversion but with the state of the international economy, which the Contadora countries themselves were feeling quite directly.

The "Soviet factor" was clearly secondary in this perspective. It was assumed that either superpower would try to put as many stones in the other's shoes as possible and that, as a consequence, just as the United States was helping the resistance in Afghanistan, the USSR would try to contribute to its rival's problems in its own immediate sphere of influence. However, "Soviet actions" were seen as clearly marginal in the explosion of the Central American conflict, not only due to the fact that there were more than enough domestic factors to account for it, but also because of the perceived marginal role that Latin America had in the context of global Soviet strategy. This was the basic disagreement in perceptions between the Contadora and the Reagan administration.

In the Contadora line of reasoning, it was not inevitable that the Central American conflict would lead to strengthening the position of the Soviet

Union in the region; actions of the other Latin American countries and the United States could help to shape outcomes. Since it was not "Cuban arms" but "Somoza" (shorthand for obsolete political structures) that explained the revolution, the only adequate way to rise to the challenge was to help to resolve the internal contradictions. Even if the solutions proposed by a given country to overcome its problems were not always to the liking of the Contadora governments, dialogue and negotiation became the two key words in the attempt to reincorporate—not eliminate—those revolutionary forces into new domestic structures that would have to be substantially overhauled. Reform was seen as unavoidable.

The implications of this alternative set of proposals were quite clear. Nicaragua was not already "lost." The inflamed anti-imperialist rhetoric of the first years was to be expected. After all, the revolutionary forces of Central America were operating on their own set of assumptions, based on the historical experience of their own countries. They were quite suspicious and skeptical of any suggestion that the U.S. government would not act as a basic supporter of the status quo and as a sworn enemy of any attempt to significantly change the obsolete realities of the subregion. This meant that Contadora needed to convince not only the United States that its ideas concerning the sources of instability in Central America were mistaken, but also the revolutionary forces in the region that their own basic understanding of U.S. behavior was inaccurate.

The Contadora nations seemed to focus on the notion that if options were kept open for Nicaragua and the Salvadoran revolutionaries *within the West*, the unavoidable process of change in the region could at least be channeled and guided in directions that would not necessarily pose real security threats to neighboring countries. Allow the revolution to loose some (understandable) pressure by letting steam out; if options are patiently kept open, the forces of the market will pull them not only toward their Latin American neighbors, but toward the United States itself.

Differences in specific policy recommendations can be traced back to this fundamental disagreement. For instance, for the Reagan administration to isolate Nicaragua economically was a rational component of a policy objective aimed at weakening and eventually overthrowing the Sandinista regime. In the eyes of Contadora this constituted a crucial mistake. If the Sandinistas were cut off from their Western option, they would accept help from any other source rather than commit suicide or abandon their revolutionary objectives. By declaring economic war on Nicaragua, the United States would only add one more building block to its own self-fulfilling prophecy of increasing Soviet involvement. And indeed, as U.S. policy unfolded over the 1983-1985 period, a sense of Greek tragedy was to permeate many Latin American analyses of the conflict.

The basic original aims of Contadora were to be shaped by these considerations. Among them, some other considerations deserve special mention:

1. To avoid the unnecessary overblowing of the Central American crisis to the global level by taking it out of the ideological framework of a friend/enemy dichotomy; the Contadora governments saw themselves as friends of the United States and that they had their own set of national interests and concerns.
2. To deal with the crisis at a regional, rather than global, level. "Latin American solutions to Latin American problems" became the motto by which that aspiration was summarized.
3. To convince both the United States and the revolutionary forces in the subregion that their basic assumptions were not adequate to deal with the realities of the crisis but rather constituted a recipe for almost unavoidable conflict.
4. Most importantly, to provide the U.S. government with an "elegant way out" of a trap of its own making that could lead to unnecessarily and dangerously overblowing the conflict to the global level. "If you are concerned with the prospects of Soviet military presence in Central America," the Contadora governments seemed to say in the first stage of their mediation, "we not only share that concern but have an adequate solution that may prevent this result at little cost."

The Evolution of the Contadora Process

In order to achieve these objectives, Contadora tried to identify several potential compromises or "deals" with which all parties could live as tolerable "second best" alternatives. Three key documents summarize the basic turning points in the process they launched: the "21 objectives" made public in September of 1983, the "Act" (proposed treaty) of September 1984, and the "Revised Act" of September 1985.

In the course of the complex negotiations of these documents the basic interests of the parties involved were clarified and the perceptions of one another's objectives were necessarily modified.

Launching the Contadora Initiative

Why was Contadora started in 1983 and, perhaps more importantly, why didn't it turn out to be a nonstarter from its very beginning? If the evaluation of interests at stake attempted in the first section of this chapter is basically correct, the answer would seem to be that the motivations behind Contadora's creation were related as much to concerns over the direction of U.S. policy under the Reagan administration as to the evolution of the Central American crisis itself.

From the beginning, the Contadora governments did not define the problem as consisting of potential collective action with the United States to deal with a common security threat. Rather, the problem was seen by the Latin Americans as one that dealt with a *possible* common threat by convincing the U.S. government not to react in ways that would create *immediate or direct* threats to their own national security.

In examining the perceptions of U.S. policy that prevailed in Latin America in late 1982 and early 1983 interesting clues to the motivations of those governments that launched the initiative emerge. Two general developments seem to be particularly relevant. The first was the seemingly increasing subregional (i.e., Central American) character and dimension of the conflict. This may be seen as the result of two closely related developments: the levels reached by the Salvadoran insurgency and the increasingly open presence of the contras in Honduras and Costa Rica. Concurrently, one saw U.S. initiatives on the military front (the *Falcon's Eye* naval and landing maneuvers in Honduras in October 1981 and the setting up of a base in Durzuna, Honduras, 25 miles from the Nicaraguan border between July and August 1982) and on the diplomatic front (the creation of the so-called Enders forum for "peace and democracy" in the second half of 1982)—initiatives that seemed to drag other Central American countries ever further into the eye of the storm.

The second development was the widening concern that the Reagan administration might, in fact, be seriously contemplating the possibility of a larger direct military intervention. The increasingly open attempts by the U.S. government to isolate Nicaragua fueled those fears, which were reinforced by the simplistic public argumentation of its spokespersons (the Kissinger report was yet to be) and the aggressive rhetoric of several high U.S. officials. As if this were not enough, fears of an explosion of subregional conflict were also fed by bilateral tensions between Nicaragua and Honduras that escalated during the same year, due in part to the increase in contra activities promoted by the United States.

Thus, the state of the Central American crisis and of U.S. policy toward the subregion during the second half of 1982 provided important incentives for Colombia, Mexico, Panama, and Venezuela to try to come up with an alternative set of policy prescriptions. The governments of Mexico and Venezuela had, in fact, previously advanced several proposals, separately and jointly, aimed at solving the crisis through diplomatic negotiations. As perceptions of threats increased, changes of government in Colombia and Mexico brought about important reevaluations of the policies pursued vis-à-vis the subregion by the previous administrations. However, other priorities in their agenda were also important in broadening the space of agreement among them. For example, the financial crisis tended to moderate Mexican positions, while similar emphasis on internal reconciliation had the opposite effect on the Colombian government.

The trend in U.S. policy during 1983 accounts for the fact that Contadora did not turn into a nonstarter after being launched in early 1983. Particularly important were the increasingly open involvement of the U.S. government in contra operations against Nicaragua and the Ahuas Taras I and II maneuvers, actions that had initiated a virtually permanent military presence by the United States in Honduras starting in early February 1983. Also troubling was the ascendancy within the U.S. administration of those officials perceived as true hard-liners when it came to Central American policies, especially after Assistant Secretary for Inter-American Affairs Thomas Enders, who seemed to have been slowly learning the complex realities of the area, was kicked upstairs to Spain.

The more complex argumentation (as compared to the original rhetoric of the administration) presented in the Kissinger Commission's report did very little to allay those concerns. The report supported precisely those aspects of U.S. policy that the Contadora countries found more disturbing. Although Contadora's original diagnosis of the crisis attached considerable importance to economic, social, and even political realities, it was the security dimension that had been their main focus. Most of the 21 "objectives" of September 1983 were directly related to that issue. Looking for an "elegant way out" for the United States by seriously taking into account its publicly stated concerns, the Contadora negotiators seemed to give clear priority to what were presumably that nation's main objectives. Thus, the United States was not only a crucial part of the circumstances helping to launch Contadora, but it was also an unavoidable presence in the deliberations. It can be argued that from its creation to the presentation of the draft agreement in September of 1984, the group worked on the assumption that the basic U.S. concerns that had to be incorporated into the text of the document were those articulated in the public statements of its officials, namely the possibility that the Soviet Union would gain a military foothold in the American continent.

As already suggested, the U.S. government was not the only actor that had to be convinced of the need to modify its original perceptions if a diplomatic solution to the crisis were to be found. The perceptions and preferences of the Central American revolutionary forces also had to be changed. In the early stages of Contadora this involved two quite different problems. The first one was the need to convince the Nicaraguan regime that it was in its interest to join a multilateral framework of diplomatic negotiation. The Sandinista government, considering itself the odd man out at the Central American ball, favored bilateral negotiations with its neighbors and with the United States. By virtue of its Latin American character, the process of Contadora took care of the first concern (negotiations with Nicaragua's neighbors), but the issue of bilateral negotiations between

Nicaragua and the United States remained open. The Nicaraguan acceptance of the multilateral framework was itself the first concession obtained from the Sandinistas. This started that regime on a road that increasingly meant choosing between lesser evils.

The second problem, which presented greater difficulties than the first, was the situation of the revolutionary movement in El Salvador. With their emphasis on security matters and intergovernmental negotiations, the early Contadora proposals left very little space for the concerns of the Salvadoran insurgents. Being a government or not being a government was clearly an important issue, and this consideration contributed to the perception that in its early moments Contadora was giving priority to the Nicaraguan revolution. In fact, the emphasis on security questions could also be interpreted as siding with the Sandinista position, which ruled out the possibility of submitting Nicaragua's internal affairs to any kind of international negotiation or supervision. The fact that the Salvadoran revolutionary movement did not issue any public criticism of a diplomatic initiative that seemed to leave it out in the cold was, in turn, as much as could have been expected.

1984: Running Ever Faster to Stay in the Same Place

Once an agreement concerning basic objectives had been hammered out in the 21 points, real business started, reaching considerable speed only in 1984. Negotiations as a solution to the Central American crisis seemed to have a chance in the context of changes in the domestic politics of the United States.

The U.S. presidential campaign of 1984 witnessed the U.S. government's adoption of a "two track" strategy. It combined increased economic and military pressure on Nicaragua and bilateral negotiations with the Sandinista regime, while maintaining a military approach to the Salvadoran insurgency. This was perceived by the Contadora group as an opportunity, and its diplomatic efforts increased in pace. Among the group's negotiators there was an almost open concern about the timetable that had to be kept. It was as if they thought that for the process to succeed it had to reach its conclusion before the first week of November, when, it was assumed, Reagan would be reelected, and in the changed political constraints of a second term presidency, would be tempted to apply a "quick fix" to the Central American crisis.

As it turned out, the "two track" strategy evolved practically concurrently with the electoral campaign. On the very same day of the election it was announced by the United States that Nicaragua was on the verge of receiving Soviet MiGs. This would have meant a significant escalation of the problem's military dimensions. The announcement itself contributed to a new climate after the presidential campaign was over, even after it became impossible for the U.S. government to sustain the original charge. In the first days of 1985 the Reagan administration unilaterally terminated its talks with the Nicaraguan government. The concerns of Latin American political observers and policymakers were borne out by reality. In the meantime, however, the Contadora process had reached its self-imposed goals, producing a quite detailed set of proposals, embodied in its 1984 draft treaty. The reactions of the different parties to the document were particularly useful in clarifying the interests at play.

The most difficult aspects in the negotiations of the document focused on two basic areas of disagreement: military/security issues (still its most important aspect) related to levels of armament, maneuvers, and military bases/installations; and domestic political issues, grouped under the general rubric of political democracy. A third set of issues that was to become important later had to do with the problems of verification of the different agreements, particularly those related to the military/security field.

The 1984 draft treaty dealt with the first two sets of issues in ways that were clearly "second best" for all parties involved. It adopted the notion of "balance" in defining the disarmament limits that should be applied to each Central American country. This meant each one's specific security needs would be taken into account in establishing their respective ceilings. It prohibited the installation of *foreign* military bases in Central America and also aimed to forbid military maneuvers in the subregion. Finally, it called for political democracy to be adopted by the Central American countries.

Initially, most observers assumed that the concessions required of Nicaragua under the document were such that the Sandinistas could hardly be expected to sign it. The other Central American countries (with the exception of El Salvador, which wanted to keep its options open) gave clear indications that they were ready to endorse the document. However, Nicaragua surprised everyone in late September by announcing that it was ready to accept the treaty as it stood. The U.S. government, caught off-guard, stated that it considered the document unacceptable only a few hours after the Nicaraguan announcement. A few days later those Central American countries that had tentatively expressed approval reversed their positions.

A document leaked from the U.S. National Security Council explained why the United States "blocked Contadora."[8] The key reasons given had to do with the problems of verification. For many Latin American observers this seemed a relatively weak argument, particularly given the fact that the agreement addressed the main stated objective of U.S. policy: the banning of Cuban and Soviet military presence in the area.

The U.S. reaction clarified two crucial points. First, it was increasingly clear that the chips that it held vis-à-vis the Central American governments gave the U.S. government virtual veto power over any multilateral exercise. Second, U.S. concerns and policy objectives needed to be reinterpreted by the Latin American nations. The treaty had prohibited a Soviet military presence and activities in the area. However, since the document spoke not of "Soviet" but of "foreign" presence and maneuvers, U.S. behavior was also restricted. The draft treaty at one and the same time forbid the USSR to enter Central America and asked the United States to leave (at least in military terms).

These developments changed the perception of the U.S. motives from the East-West rivalry (which at least has some potential to elicit common concerns with the United States from the governments of Latin America) to that of preserving U.S. hegemony (which brought the game to the entirely different court of national interests and concerns). Even if avoiding a Soviet presence was accepted as the basic aim of U.S. policy, the behavior of the U.S. government seemed to indicate quite clearly that it perceived the maintenance of a direct veto power over the area's developments as the only way to effectively guarantee such an outcome. Hegemony was, for all practical purposes, the operational objective of U.S. policy in Central America.

This development presented the Contadora countries with a difficult task. On the one hand, it appeared that they needed to recognize the ultimate veto power of the United States, not only by accommodating U.S. concerns about the Soviet presence, but also by legitimizing and formalizing a continued presence of the United States. The issue was how far that accommodation would have to go. The very survival of the Sandinista government seemed to be unacceptable to the United States. If such was the case, the notion of negotiations seemed irrelevant unless the Sandinistas could be expected to negotiate their own demise. The United States was perceived to have gone from a game of "bully" to one of "big bully" in its "negotiating strategy."[9] In fact, it seemed that anything that was acceptable to the Sandinista government would be immediately unacceptable to the Reagan administration.

The Revised Act of 1985: Anything to Make You Happy

Accommodating U.S. concerns led to important changes in the 1985 version of the Contadora treaty. In the first place, the notion of "parity" was chosen in defining acceptable levels of armaments in each country, instead of the principle of particular needs. As a consequence, Nicaragua's claim of being the "odd-man-out" (i.e., that it faced the possibility of conflict with more than one army at the same time) was downgraded. Maneuvers were not to be prohibited, but rather, "regulated" (in which instance, bases slipped through the back door), and the proposals directed at the internal politics of Central American countries were more clearly aimed at "national reconciliation." This drew parallels between the situations of all those countries in the region in which there were armed conflicts and thus questioned the Sandinista claim that the Sandinistas faced a situation of external aggression and not a civil war.

Nicaragua considered the concessions made to the U.S. government too great and established as a precondition that the United States commit itself to the treaty by signing an additional protocol. Without such a commitment the Sandinistas feared that the restrictions put on them by the 1985 treaty would become one more arrow with which the U.S. government would attempt to bleed the Sandinista revolution in anticipation of a more drastic "final solution."

In addition to its transformed perceptions of U.S. policy aims, there were two other developments that altered the Contadora group's approach to the mediation process after the 1984 treaty's failure. The basic cost/benefit analysis of the group's original members changed. On the cost side, the intensification of their financial worries made the real or potential costs of the initiative increasingly difficult to bear. The potential benefits to be gained, in particular the avoidance of even costlier alternatives, were lessened as the perception arose that the U.S. government had postponed consideration of direct military intervention in favor of "low intensity warfare." This put the motor of the initiative almost in neutral.

The second new factor was the creation of the Lima support group in the summer of 1985. Up to that moment the countries whose immediate national concerns were at stake had carried the weight of the initiative. However, if "low intensity conflict" made the possibility of direct military intervention less immediate, it also added a new element to the equation: the almost completely open disregard on the part of the superpower of the basic principles and rules of international life.

It was this fact that provided new common ground to old and new participants—participants, as has been already pointed out, that were facing domestic political situations in which such considerations were becoming more relevant. Nicaragua's initiatives aimed at involving the "new democracies" of the southern cone were also important. As if moved by a clear understanding of the basic logic described above, the Sandinistas seemed openly concerned with the prospect that, in its attempts to accommodate U.S. interests, Contadora would end up standing on its head, transformed into a new element of North American strategy. One way to make this less likely was by involving a new circle of credible and impartial witnesses in the negotiations.

At first, however, the addition of this new set of participants did little to change what appeared to be an almost unavoidable logic from unfolding. A document was presented that, in the opinion of the Nicaraguan government, went too far in its attempts to accommodate the United States. This brought Contadora to its worst impasse, and soon Nicaragua requested that the process be put on hold for a six-month period.

In the following months, helped by the inauguration of a new Guatemalan government and by the stand that it took in the Central American crisis, the Nicaraguan request was dropped and the search for a compromise was intensified. What was to become the "Group of Eight" tried to convince all the parties involved to make concessions. The group visited all the Central American capitals and Washington as well. The results, however, were quite meager. When a new version of the treaty was presented in mid-1986, only the Nicaraguan government formally responded to it. The military alternative, embodied in the "low intensity" strategy seemed to be well under way. The U.S. decision to overthrow the Sandinista government became increasingly clear. The Contadora countries, their most basic fears removed by the new U.S. strategy and disenchanted at what they saw as a lack of political will on the part of the Central American governments, became increasingly aloof. Nicaragua's isolation grew, and the self-fulfilling prophecy of increased Soviet presence quickly unfolded. As a result, the prospects for any regional diplomatic solution to the crisis dimmed.

In October 1986, when the prospects for a negotiated settlement seemed to be at the lowest point since the beginning of the conflict, new domestic political developments in the United States opened possibilities. As the first rumblings of "Contragate" emerged, Central American actors began repositioning themselves, and peaceful solutions were again considered thinkable.

This time it was the new Costa Rican government that took the initiative. It is difficult to think of another participant that was more clearly in a position to deal with the new emphasis of U.S. demands. The so-called "Arias plan" was presented as being a part of the more general context of the Contadora initiative. With it, however, the focus moved from the security questions associated with original U.S. public statements to the very nature of the Nicaraguan revolution.

A final point has to be made regarding the key obstacles that the Contadora process faced. The "regional" or even subregional diplomatic solution was not the only "diplomatic" solution open to the United States. Even if its confrontational strategy failed, it could still try to "strike a deal" with precisely the actor that it said it wanted excluded in the first place. The Soviet Union had very little to offer at the beginning of the game. However, at the same time that Western options had been cut off for Nicaragua and the Sandinista regime had been increasingly motivated to look for support in the socialist camp, the Soviets had seen an increase in the number and quality of their chips as well as in their incentives to placate the United States. As a result, it might have been possible for the United States to negotiate with the USSR so that Nicaragua's lifelines would be cut. This would, however, have been be a different ball game, where many other "global issues" would have played a part.

If this had happened, a chagrined smile might have set on the faces of Latin American political leaders. A crucial issue for the future of this hemisphere would not have been dealt with by them, but by the "real actors" of international politics. They would not be happy with the result, but they would see as a paradox of paradoxes the picture of the Soviets having a say in what was originally conceptualized by them as a Latin American affair. Instead of simply taking the Central American crisis out of the Latin American sphere and bringing it to the hemispheric one, the Reagan administration would have validated its own view of the world at the expense of the interests of its Latin American neighbors and those of its own country as well.

Conclusions: Some Basic Lessons of the Contadora Experience

The basic lesson of the Contadora experience for the prospects of collective security in the Americas are best understood if one deals separately with the question of intra-Latin American cooperation and inter-American collaboration. As regards the first issue, it is necessary to underline the basic characteristics of the Contadora experience. Several doubts can be raised regarding the eventual results of the decision to institutionalize the Group of Eight. In the first place, it should be said that the informality and institutional flexibility of the Contadora process allowed for creativity and dynamism. This was the result of a basic reality of the experience: Latin American countries acted together when they perceived a clear threat to their shared geographic interests. Contadora was not an expression of any kind of ethereal Latin American solidarity based on common language, culture, or history.

The important addition of the Lima support group stressed the vitality of very old principles, first developed precisely in the context of relations with the United States during the first decades of the Pan American movement. In and of itself, however, the interest in the defense of those principles could hardly have provided the motivation needed to be willing to pay the costs associated with moving the initiative forward. The Contadora experience clearly suggests that the existence of strong motivations on the part of its initial members was what kept the process moving. Even the motivations of other Latin American actors were clearly influenced by the strong commitment of the original four. In fact, some of the Lima group nations participated in spite of the relatively minor role that the Central American crisis had in their own foreign policy priorities, doing so not only because it befitted their status as Latin America's "influentials" or because of their opposition to unprincipled and unlawful policies, but because it was also a way to lay a claim to the support of the middle-powers of the region when their own national interests might be at stake in the future.

The basic lesson to be drawn from all this is that in the near future Latin American countries can only be expected to play the joint activist role like that of Contadora if they share a clear perception of a threat to their own interests. In all likelihood, this requirement will be reinforced by the sheer number and size of the problems that Latin American governments will be facing in their own domestic policy agendas and foreign relations (such as financial issues and bilateral dealings with the United States).

What may be expected is a situation wherein changing groupings of Latin American countries will emerge to deal with situations they perceive as common threats, which may not necessarily be shared by other countries of the area. The role of the Group of Eight may be twofold under those circumstances. It may clarify the basic principles with which any and all of those more particular groupings will have to comply to gain the support of the rest of the region. It might also provide a core group for those instances of cooperation in which a particular subset of its members (for example, those whose direct interest would seem to be at stake) would take prime responsibility. The very fact that the Group of Eight includes representatives of practically all subregions of Latin America, except for the Caribbean, could be seen as providing interesting possibilities in that regard.

However, the experience of Contadora also provides some lessons that raise doubts as to the likelihood that such an institutionalized core group may become truly effective. There is the potential for the group to be perceived as creating a "two-tiered" arrangement for the other countries of the area. Maybe this could be mitigated if some form of subregional representation could be arranged. This, however, would not change the crucial fact that those countries dissatisfied with the structure or workings of a given arrangement could always look for alternatives beyond such structures. If the United States were to not agree to abide by those Latin American arrangements, such alternatives would be nearby. This is partly what had happened in the context of the Central American crisis. When the question for the Central American countries, other than Nicaragua, was reduced to choosing the tutelage of either the United States or the Contadora countries, the pragmatic consideration regarding which potential suitors had more to offer colored many decisions. In that situation the Contadora countries faced very tough competition. However, the fact that the governments of Costa Rica, El Salvador, and Honduras refrained from openly questioning the Contadora effort and squarely joining the Reagan administration may indicate that even for them the price of a more direct military alternative on the part of the United States was too high.

A final implication for collective security arrangements on the hemispheric level is basically that possible *U.S. actions* galvanized the whole process. This is a reminder that the most immediate threats to Latin American security many times do not come from the East but from the North.

Where does all this lead us concerning the question of collective security in the Americas? Perhaps the most important point to keep in mind is that, at least during the first stages of the Contadora process, there was a fundamental incompatibility of Contadora's proposals and policy aims with the key operational objective of the Reagan administration in Central America, namely that of guaranteeing its hegemony, or if one prefers a different language, its veto power over developments in the area. In the eyes of several U.S. officials the key question seems to have been quite simple: Why put the basic responsibility for maintaining stability in its historical mare nostrum in anybody else's hands? The Latin American governments were defeated by an actor that could mobilize more resources in support of its own preferred *national* options. And this, to say the least, does not provide the best of grounds for the creation of any inter-American collective security arrangement. Common perceptions of common threats that would allow for such an option do not seem to exist. As a result, it is more probable that most efforts to collectively deal with security threats in the near future will tend to be Latin American in nature. The most likely exception will focus on those smaller Latin American states, in particular those in Central America and the Caribbean, which may tend to choose protectors with more concrete resources; this option may only be open, however, to those states that are in a priority area for the superpower.

If the most likely future is one of Latin American initiatives in the security field, what, then, will be the role of inter-American relations? Two quite distinct possibilities present themselves. One possible configuration of inter-American relations can be imagined if one assumes that the policies of the Reagan administration did reflect *national* interests. In that case, Latin American nations would concentrate on areas where the possibility of a direct conflict with U.S. priorities is less probable and "regional responsibility" more realistic. The temptation then would be very great to accept the principle that the Caribbean and Central America constitute North American "preserves."[10] With Central America and the Caribbean eventually back under clear U.S. tutelage and South American governments developing their own subregional groupings, the middle-powers of Contadora could end up quite isolated. The borderline status of Colombia and Venezuela in geopolitical terms may give them some breathing space. However, Mexico would be put in an extremely uncomfortable position: that of a lost pariah in a society of restricted and increasingly interwoven subregional collective security arrangements.

A second version of future inter-American relations would be one in which the United States and Latin American nations find their national interests to be compatible and therefore joint action feasible. The Contadora experience shows that in those areas of high priority for the United States, where it may perceive its own interests to be directly at stake, it will be extremely difficult to advance Latin American security objectives in direct opposition to the United States. Given the needs of the economies of the subregion and the restrictions of their capabilities (financial and other), the problem will not be whether or not to have a U.S. presence, but what kind of a presence to have. Forms of joint action would be necessary in that situation. One of the most patent lessons of the experience is the need to "strike a deal." This, however, may be possible only if the United States moderates its maximalist demands and thereby allows the debate to shift from the level of conflicting national interests to that of shared common concerns.

Is there a possibility for a less maximalist set of policy preferences by the United States? To answer this question, it helps to recall the basic distinctions between the interests of the Lima support group and those of the original Contadora group: While the latter group of nations saw the conflict in Central America as a threat to their *national* interests, the Lima group's members saw it as primarily involving their *governmental* interests. Were the policies pursued by the Reagan administration related to truly *national* interests, or were they basically *governmental;* that is, the preferences of the administration and the particular segment of U.S. public opinion it represented? If they truly represented *national* interests one would be hard pressed to be optimistic. However, if important aspects of those policies did not reflect a national consensus but could be altered by a different administration, the potential for a deal may be there. The policies pursued in its first year in office by the Bush administration—which is after all, of the same party as its predecessor—toward the Nicaraguan, and, more generally, the Central American, situation still do not allow for a definite answer to this question.

Notes

1. James R. Kurth, "The United States, Latin America and the World: The Changing International Context of U.S.-Latin American Relations" in *The United States and Latin America in the 1980's*, ed. Kevin J. Middlebrook and Carlos Rico (Pittsburgh: University of Pittsburgh Press, 1986).

2. For short presentations of those Latin American attempts, as viewed from different North American perspectives, see James D. Theberge, *Latin America in the World System: The Limits of Internationalism* (Beverly Hills: Sage, 1975), and Abraham Lowenthal and Albert Fishlow, *Latin America's Emergence: Towards a U.S. Response* (New York: Foreign Policy Association, 1979).

3. I do not intend to downplay the relevance of certain developments that brought about changes in security perceptions. Rather I hope to put them in context. For instance, extremely important events, such as the Falklands/Malvinas war, were more expressions of the new realities than a cause of changes in security perceptions. The ultimate source of change had much deeper roots. In the Falklands/Malvinas case, an emerging power—one of those new realities—engaged in military confrontation with another *Western* country over a very old problem: nationalistic claims of territorial sovereignty.

4. My intention in using such language is to draw a clear distinction, in terms of policies historically pursued by the United States, between the countries of Central America and the Caribbean on the one hand, and those of South America on the other.

The first group has not only received a disproportionate share of U.S. military actions in the region, but it constitutes a clearly different case in terms of actual military presence and installations as well as acknowledged influence in the internal political affairs of the subregion. See, for the innumerable illustrations one could use, Walter LaFeber, *Inevitable Revolutions: The United States in Central America* (New York: W. W. Norton & Company, 1984).

5. See, for example, the account of U.S. participation in the 1954 coup in Guatemala presented by Stephen Schlesinger and Stephen Kinzer in *Bitter Fruit* (Garden City, New York: Anchor Books, 1983).

6. Jeane Kirkpatrick, "Dictatorships and Double Standards," *Commentary* 68, no. 5 (November 1979): 43. Emphasis mine.

7. *Report of the President's National Bipartisan Commission on Central America* (New York: Macmillan, 1984).

8. Alma Guillermoprieto and David Hoffman, "Document Describes How U.S. 'Blocked' A Contadora Treaty," *The Washington Post*, November 6, 1984, p. 1.

9. Glenn H. Snyder and Paul Diesing, *Conflict Among Nations* (Princeton: Princeton University Press, 1977), pp. 46–47, 53–54, and 122–124. I am indebted to Patrick Barrett for having brought to my attention the relevance of the "bully" model in this connection.

10. General Edgardo Mercado Jarrín, interview with author, Lima, Peru, May 14, 1987.

7

Suppressing the Interventionist Impulse: Toward a New Collective Security System in the Americas

Richard J. Bloomfield

In the 1980s, as a result of the Reagan administration's policies in Central America, the issue of U.S. intervention once again came to the forefront of U.S.-Latin American relations. Although this book was inspired by the authors' concern about the effects of those policies, its purpose has not been to revive the polemic over Nicaragua. Intervention is, after all, an old wound that periodically gets reopened; the Contra War is only a recent abrasion. Rather, the authors' goal has been to examine U.S. intervention in Latin America as a phenomenon of long standing and to explore the possibilities of a more effective alternative. Such an approach would take the form of a new effort at collective security in the Americas, but one that, unlike past attempts, would succeed in suppressing the "interventionist impulse."[1]

This concluding chapter attempts to tie together the arguments presented in the preceding pages by doing three things:

1. Showing that the United States can no longer afford unilateral intervention in Latin America, and therefore that the creation of a viable collective security system is an urgent task.
2. Analyzing the roots of the interventionist impulse that has characterized U.S. policy toward Latin America in this century, in order to determine how formidable a stumbling block it might be to a new attempt at collective security.
3. Describing the elements of a collective security regime that might forestall unilateral U.S. intervention by taking advantage of new circumstances in the hemisphere and in world politics to square the circle of differing U.S. and Latin American security concerns.

A Troubled Relationship

As seen by Latin Americans, their enduring problem has been how to cope with the greater power of the United States: how to benefit from it and how to avoid being dominated by it. For North Americans, the problem has been how to prevent their enemies from using the weakness of Latin American political institutions to threaten the U.S. national interest. Typically, the enemy has been a European great power that appears to be outflanking the United States through its "soft underbelly."

These two views of the relationship arise from the respective positions of the United States and Latin America in what James Kurth calls the Atlantic Triangle. As Kurth shows, the two perspectives can only be reconciled if the United States could meet Latin American needs for internal security and economic benefits; if not, what he calls the "deep structure" of the relationship holds within it the seeds of conflict.[2]

With the rise of the United States in the twentieth century to the position of the world's leading power and the concomitant growth in the intensity and scope of its relations with Latin America, this latent conflict has become a frequent reality. The Latin American countries have simultaneously pressed the United States to concede them greater economic benefits, while resisting the natural tendency of a neighboring Great Power to shape or restrict their political autonomy. For its part, the United States has found it difficult to square its role as a power that has global responsibilities and interests with a policy of according Latin America special treatment. At the same time, the perceived threat to its national security from a rival European power—most recently the Soviet Union—has prompted the United States with some regularity to practice the ultimate form of political interference in the affairs of Latin American states—the overt or covert use of armed force. The result, as Muñoz points out in his chapter in this book, is that the United States has come to be viewed in Latin America as *the* interventionist power in the hemisphere. In effect, the issue of intervention has become the leitmotiv of the U.S.-Latin American relationship, the issue that colors discourse about all others.

The Vulnerable Giant

For most of its history, the United States has been able to ignore, or at least been willing to bear, the condemnation from Latin America that its acts of intervention have produced. Latin America's vulnerability to the United States has been great; the reverse has not been true. Early in the twentieth century, the United States became Latin America's principal trading partner and source of capital; in contrast, Latin America has been a secondary market for U.S. exports and investments. Nor has Latin America been able to look elsewhere to counter U.S. interventionist impulses. After World War II, neither Western Europe nor Japan had reason to challenge U.S. political primacy in the Western Hemisphere. For a Latin American country to attempt to use the Soviet Union as a counterweight to the United States was to risk the very U.S. intervention such a move sought to prevent.

It has become commonplace to point out that the hegemony over Latin America that the United States enjoyed in the two decades after World War II has been eroded as a result of the resurgence of Europe and Japan and the relative decline of the economic power of the United States. Yet, measured by traditional criteria, the balance of power between the United States and Latin America continues to be overwhelmingly in favor of the United States. The oil boom of the 1970s for a time provided Mexico and Venezuela with resources to pursue independent regional policies, but the boom has long since collapsed. While Japanese and European investment and trade have become significant for many Latin American countries, the United States still accounts for 40 percent of the area's exports and imports. U.S. banks hold about 20 percent of the region's staggering burden of debt.[3] The wave of optimism about national regeneration that swept Latin America with the return of democracy to most of the region in the early 1980s has all but evaporated; the decade's chronic economic crisis has tarnished the luster of yesterday's democratic heroes and has sharpened domestic political conflict. U.S. hegemony may be eroding, but any announcement of its demise would appear to be premature.

Yet, for all that, something *has* changed. In spite of its power, the United States has become more vulnerable to events and trends in Latin America than at any previous time in its history.

It has long been understood that the technological revolutions of the modern era have produced an unprecedented ability in advanced societies to penetrate weaker ones. What has been less readily recognized is that the penetration is no longer one-way. Paradoxically, the more technologically advanced the society, the more open it may be to influences from the rest of the world, particularly if its political culture places a high value on the freedom of movement of people, goods, and information. This has become the reality in the United States' relationship with Latin America. The drug epidemic in the U.S. inner cities, the stresses of absorbing large numbers of immigrants, the shrinkage of traditional export markets, and the overexposure of the U.S. banking system to foreign debtors all are evidence of an unprecedented vulnerability to Latin America. Even some of the emerging threats to the environment are originating south of the border: the warming trend in the earth's climate has its origin in the destruction of Brazilian rain forests, as well as in the automobile exhausts of American cities of both continents.

To be sure, like the traditional security threats of the past, this vulnerability stems from Latin American weakness, not strength. What is novel, however, is that it is a type of vulnerability against which gunboats are of little use. The preponderant power of the United States that has served for the better part of a century to confirm Secretary of State Richard Olney's proclamation of 1895 that "the United States is practically sovereign on this continent and its fiat is law"[4] is no longer effective in warding off the dangers from these new sources. As Stanley Hoffmann has observed, sovereignty no longer means the ability to project authority abroad, but only the authority "to cope with a host of external penetrations, obstacles, and constraints."[5] If the United States is to cope with the external penetrations emanating from Latin America and the Caribbean, it needs a strategy that emphasizes cooperation and compromise, and that makes the Latin Americans part of the solution rather than part of the problem.

The Weakness of Unilateralism

There is, however, a strong and persistent strain of unilateralism in the U.S. approach to the world: a conviction that the country can face down threats from abroad, if only its leaders have the determination to take tough measures to force recalcitrant foreigners to behave. This belief was a cardinal tenet of the administration that took office in 1981. Capitalizing on the frustration of the nation at setbacks in various corners of the world during the 1970s, the Reagan administration espoused an approach to international affairs—dubbed global internationalism by its defenders—that emphasized the use of U.S. military power to confound enemies, a distrust of negotiation, and a disdain for multilateralism.

In Latin America, the administration's unilateralism was displayed most notoriously in its approach to the conflicts in Central America, but it carried over to other kinds of issues as well. Thus, the United States threatened to "de-certify" Latin American countries that were not deemed to be sufficiently zealous in carrying out U.S.-designed antinarcotics programs and insisted that the only solution to the debt crisis was the adoption by the debtor countries of draconian economic targets that would have been unacceptable to the creditor countries own citizenry.

The weakness of unilateralism is twofold. First, it attempts to project on societies that have very different values and social structures from ours a model of behavior derived from U.S. experience. The circumstances of the Latin American states' historical formation have in most cases produced polities that are weak and divided. This makes it doubly difficult for their governments to cope with ruthless drug dealers, to offer their peoples the economic opportunities that would keep them at home, or to carry out austere economic policies. But the unrealistic premise of unilateralism is that if we threaten these societies with sanctions of various sorts they will somehow mend their ways, even if it requires rooting out deeply embedded attitudes and overturning the existing social and political order.

The second weakness of unilateralism is that it is, more often than not, simply scapegoating. Certifying Latin American governments' performance in combating drug trafficking, aside from being demeaning, ignores the dismal record of the United States in reducing its own population's appetite for drugs; demanding that these countries shoulder the entire burden of adjusting to the debt crisis disregards U.S. complicity in creating the crisis in the first place. Such hypocrisy produces resentment and recrimination, which are hardly conducive to cooperation.

The End of Intervention?

In creating and sustaining the Nicaraguan insurgency, the Reagan administration was reverting to the ultimate form of unilateralism. The effect of the contra policy in Latin America was predictable. It revived an image of the United States as the bully of the hemisphere, an image that had been softened by the efforts of President Carter to build a new relationship with the Latin American people based on respect for sovereignty (the Panama Canal treaties) and opposition to repression (the human rights policy). At home, the contra policy aroused intense opposition and, in fact, the majority of U.S. citizens consistently opposed it. Perhaps worst of all, it diverted the attention and energies of leaders in Washington from the urgent problems that will do more to affect the future well-being of both halves of the hemisphere than anything that is likely to happen in Central America. These problems—debt, trade and investment, migration, drugs, the environment—require sustained high level attention, a concept of U.S. interests that commands public support, and an unprecedented degree of inter-American cooperation. This implies a sharp departure from the unilateralist policies of the 1980s.

The last decade of the century may prove to be a propitious time for such a sea change in U.S. policy toward Latin America. As the Cold War winds down, one might expect the issue of intervention to fade into the background, as in fact it has at times in the past when extrahemispheric threats have abated. Yet intervention has risen phoenix-like in the midst of other grand attempts at inter-American cooperation. One need only recall the days of the Alliance for Progress. Before we enthusiastically consign the Reagan Doctrine to the ashbin of history, we need to examine the deep roots of intervention in this country's historical experience.

The Roots of Intervention

The interventionist impulse had its origins, ironically, in the dangers faced by the new and weak American republic from attempts by the Great Powers of

Europe to intervene in the affairs of the North American continent. The ink was hardly dry on the Treaty of Paris of 1783 when problems began with the British, who refused to evacuate their garrisons on U.S. territory and intrigued with Indians and white separatists. In the forty years between the end of the Revolutionary War and the proclamation of President Monroe's famous doctrine, U.S. leaders faced what must have seemed relentless pressures from Europe. The history of that period is that of a series of such challenges: to define the new nation's boundaries and make them secure against the arc of British, Spanish, and French territories surrounding them; to escape from French attempts to turn its wartime ally into a permanent satellite by meddling in U.S. internal politics; to cope with British bullying on the high seas; and to forestall the victorious anti-Napoleonic alliance from reasserting European control over the newly independent Spanish colonies. By virtue of considerable luck and skillful diplomacy, the young republic not only survived but pushed its boundaries far to the West. This long effort imprinted a lesson indelibly on the American psyche, however, a lesson that was crystallized in the Monroe Doctrine: attempts by European Powers to gain control over parts of the New World threaten the national interest of the United States and must be resisted.[6]

Ideology and Security

From the beginning, this strategic premise encompassed more than resistance to the acquisition of territory by a European power. The Founding Fathers were acutely conscious that their new country was not just another sovereign state with a demarcated territory and population; it was above all a new idea, a political system founded on very different principles from those of the European states. The Europeans were quite open in their disdain for, and distrust of, that new system. It is no wonder that the first generations of U.S. leaders viewed European control or even influence over parts of the Americas not only as a threat to their country's expansion but as potential outposts of hostile political principles, bases of operations for those that would like to see their experiment fail. Thus, in his message of 1823, Monroe, addressing the indications that the Quadruple Alliance was contemplating helping Spain reestablish its dominion over its former colonies, warned "It is impossible that the allied powers should extend their *political system* to any portion of either continent without endangering our peace and happiness (emphasis added)."[7]

This is not to deny that the desire for more territory was at times the motive for the invocation of the Monroe Doctrine. Looking at the nineteenth century, it is difficult to separate its two strands: expansion and ideology. U.S. Presidents from Polk onward invoked Monroe's principles in the face of threats that European powers might acquire colonies or satellites that would block U.S. aspirations to become a continental republic.[8] Indeed, in the administration of Theodore Roosevelt, the doctrine stood almost entirely for old-fashioned, European-style imperialism. Roosevelt and his friends were obsessed with America's destiny to join the ranks of the Great Powers; Roosevelt's corollary to the doctrine, which proclaimed the U.S. as the policeman of the Caribbean, was designed to prevent European encroachments in the area that could threaten the canal under construction in Panama and hinder the ascendancy of U.S. naval power.

In many ways, however, the administration of the first Roosevelt, rather than ushering in the twentieth century, epitomized the culmination of Manifest Destiny and the nineteenth century process of territorial expansion. In the intensely ideological twentieth century, the preoccupation of the Founding Fathers with the threat of alien political systems once again came to dominate U.S. thinking about Latin America. The policy of Woodrow Wilson, in which idealism and realism coexisted, rather than that of Theodore Roosevelt, was the precursor of the modern era.

Wilson intervened in Mexico in 1914 to "teach the Latin American republics to elect good men," as he later intervened in Europe to make the world "safe for democracy." However, with the outbreak of war in Europe a few months after the U.S. landing at Vera Cruz, Wilson's policy toward Mexico became less concerned about elections and more with preventing Imperial Germany from gaining a foothold there. Like FDR twenty years later, Wilson sought to bolster an ascendant Mexican leader as a way of thwarting German attempts to make trouble between the two countries. This pragmatism led him to terminate the two military interventions into Mexico that occurred during his first term.[9]

At the same time, Wilson sent U.S. marines to Haiti in 1915 and to the Dominican Republic the following year to bring law and order out of civil strife, thus carrying forward de facto protectorates established under Presidents Theodore Roosevelt and William Howard Taft that were designed to prevent Germany from using instability in the Caribbean to obtain bases there. These occupations took on a life of their own, however, and lasted well beyond the defeat of Germany, as did a similar occupation of Nicaragua.

By the early 1930s U.S. leaders were disillusioned with their role as political tutors to the people of Central America and the island nations of the Caribbean who stubbornly refused to adopt more than the outward forms of democracy. Moreover, there was now no threat from a hostile European power to justify such intervention. The Hoover administration began the liquidation of U.S. intervention in the Caribbean basin, largely in response to its unpopularity at home. What Hoover began, the second Roosevelt made the cornerstone of his Latin American policy. Roosevelt completed the withdrawal of U.S. forces from the Caribbean, and in 1933 and again in 1936

the United States, in an inter-American convention and protocol ratified by
the U.S. Senate, accepted a sweeping prohibition against the intervention of
one American state in the affairs of another.

By the mid-1930s, however, what began as retrenchment in response to
domestic pressures became a national security strategy. FDR had become
concerned about the growing menace of Nazi Germany and placed a high
priority on shoring up relations with the countries on the U.S. southern flank.
The nonintervention policy paid off, and in a series of agreements that
culminated in the postwar Rio Treaty, the Latin Americans joined the United
States in a full-fledged collective security system. Thus, Roosevelt struck a
kind of "great bargain" with Latin America—nonintervention in exchange for
collective security.[10]

The Breakdown of the Collective Security Bargain

In the aftermath of World War II and with the advent of the Cold War, FDR's
"great bargain" was undone by a series of interventions, beginning in
Guatemala in 1954. At first, an attempt was made to preserve the appearance
of nonintervention by the use of proxies—rebellions ostensibly led by
Guatemalans or Cubans but organized and directed by the CIA—but as the
threat from an expansionary Soviet Union seemed to intensify, even the
pretense of U.S. noninvolvement was dropped, as in the Dominican Republic
in 1965, Nicaragua in the 1980s, and Grenada in 1984. In the early 1960s, the
United States briefly made an effort to enlist Latin America in collective
action against Cuba, and was partly successful thanks to the attempts of the
Cubans to subvert a number of their neighbors. The prospects of large-scale
economic assistance through the Alliance for Progress also buttressed the
anti-Castro coalition for a few years.

Yet the U.S. commitment to collective security was only skin-deep: the
decade began with the Bay of Pigs; the Dominican intervention marked its
midpoint, and it closed with the efforts of the Nixon administration to
promote a coup in Chile to prevent Salvador Allende from becoming
president. In the 1970s, the attempt by Jimmy Carter to base his Latin
American policy on nonintervention was muddied by the use of U.S. power
to pressure authoritarian regimes to stop the abuse of human rights and was
challenged by the Nicaraguan revolution at the end of his term. The Reagan
administration at least was clear in its own mind about intervention. Driven
by its obsession with the Soviet Union as the source of all evil in the world, it
adopted a frankly interventionist policy in Central America and the
Caribbean.

The National Security Doctrine

In the context of 1823, the Monroe Doctrine was a defensive policy, aimed at warding off European intervention. The problem has been its evolution over time into an interventionist doctrine, particularly reinforced in the postwar era by what Robert Pastor has described earlier in this book as the "National Security Perspective."[11] The National Security Perspective can be summarized in the following syllogism: (1) if the Soviet Union were able to use another Western Hemisphere state, particularly one in the Caribbean area, as a base of military operations, it could gain a strategic advantage over the United States; (2) if Marxist-Leninist movements seize power in Latin America or the Caribbean, they inevitably will align themselves with the Soviet Union; at the worst, they will then provide the Soviets with military facilities, at the least, they will act as Soviet proxies in destabilizing their neighbors, eventually surrounding the United States with Soviet bases for military and intelligence operations; (3) therefore, Marxist-Leninist movements must be prevented from taking power, or overthrown if they succeed in doing so.

There are a number of things wrong with this syllogism. One weakness has been the lack of discrimination in its application: interventions were undertaken on the basis of the flimsiest of evidence that Marxist-Leninists were in the process of seizing power. Examples include the Guatemala case in 1954, in which a U.S.-sponsored "insurgency" was prompted by reports that a few communists had gained positions of influence in the Arbenz government and that that government had acquired some Czech arms in response to the threat of an exile invasion, and the Dominican intervention of 1965, when it was alleged that the "Constitutionalist" forces calling for the return of Juan Bosch to power would pave the way for a "Castro-Communist" takeover.

The syllogism's most fundamental flaw, however, is that its minor premise is false. Especially since the Cuban Missile Crisis, the assumption that the triumph of Marxist-Leninists inevitably leads to a worsening of the strategic balance badly exaggerates the likelihood that such regimes will risk their survival by accepting Soviet offensive weapons or that the Soviets would again engage in such a provocative act. It also writes off the use of political and diplomatic instruments in checking the impulses of the new revolutionary regime to subvert its neighbors. The result is the operational conclusion that the only effective way to deal with Marxist regimes in Latin America is to overthrow them.[12] Thus, the reaction of the Nixon administration to the election of Allende and of the Reagan administration to the Sandinistas and to the New Jewel Government in Grenada was the dubious proposition that U.S. security could only be safeguarded by the downfall of these regimes.

Even in the case of Cuba, where, as Jorge Domínguez points out in his chapter, there is ample evidence that Castro was determined to be hostile to the United States from the start, it is questionable that it was necessary to deal with the potential trouble he represented in 1961 by attempting to overthrow him. What is a fact is that the Missile Crisis followed the Bay of Pigs, not vice versa.

It is hard to escape the conclusion that U.S. reactions to Latin American revolutionaries have been more the function of the ideology of the revolutionaries than their actual or even potential strategic importance. How can we explain the persistent obsession of U.S. policymakers with ideology?

Ideology and the American Experience

For the answers to that question, one must turn back to the conviction of the Founding Fathers that theirs was an embattled experiment facing a hostile world. These early concerns were later reinforced by the phenomenon of immigration. De Tocqueville was perhaps the first to point out that their democratic institutions are the only thing that all U.S. citizens have in common—the one bond among them all. Lacking the ties that serve to unify other nations—race, ethnicity, religion—Americans' common tie is their democratic political system, which promises them freedom and equality. Freedom from tyranny and the bonds of the class system were not sacred just to the early settlers; they have been the magnet that has drawn immigrants throughout the history of the United States. The Europeans that flooded into the United States in the nineteenth and early twentieth centuries, like their Anglo-Saxon predecessors, left Europe to escape tyranny or to improve their economic situation. Hence, patriotism in the United States takes the form of devotion to the country's political institutions, not, as in Europe, to the race, the tribe-as-nation, the state, or the "land." If the identity of the nation is found in its political institutions, then whatever threatens those institutions is a threat to the nation itself. There is perhaps no other country in which there is such a complete identification of its political system with the integrity of the nation as in the United States of America.[13]

This explains why U.S. citizens have always been so sensitive to the spread of antidemocratic ideologies among their neighbors in this hemisphere. Most Latin American dictators have, in fact, espoused no ideology or have paid lip service to democratic ideals. Until the recent concern with human rights, such traditional *caudillos* drew little attention in the United States. Not so with authoritarian Latin American regimes that based their legitimacy on antidemocratic ideologies, particularly when these ideologies were linked to European powers, as U.S. reactions to such otherwise diverse regimes as those of Maximilian, Perón, Castro, and the

Sandinistas demonstrate.

U.S. policy has never been "isolationist" in the Western Hemisphere. The debate between isolationists and interventionists earlier in this century was a debate about policy toward Europe alone, and it was settled by World War II. Americans' experience in that conflict, however, did serve to deepen their traditional belief that the country's security required regimes in the Americas that were either democratic or, at least, nonideological.

Americans drew three important lessons from World War II. The first lesson was that technological advances in waging war had given hostile powers anywhere in the world the capability of striking at the United States directly; that finished off the isolationists, whose case rested largely on the protection afforded by the Atlantic Ocean. The second lesson reinforced U.S. fear of antidemocratic ideologies: the Nazi and communist movements had a universalist zealotry that made the Holy Alliance's ambition a century before to restore the monarchical principle seem feeble by comparison. The third lesson was the "Lesson of Munich," which was that totalitarian aggressors must be confronted early, when they begin their drive for world domination, lest the fall of one "domino" lead to the fall of another, and so on.

The Lesson of Munich came to be applied universally by the national security strategists of the Cold War. By the end of the Truman administration, those who saw the United States as globally vulnerable and U.S. security interests as a seamless web had vanquished those who would have applied containment on a selective basis.[14] Although they talked the language of power politics, the globalists' case at bottom was ideological: it assumed that successful communist revolutions, regardless of their location on the globe or the circumstances in which they arose, were a threat to American freedoms. Thus was the traditional fear of the incursion of alien ideologies into the Western Hemisphere powerfully reinforced by the Cold War.

The consensus for a policy of global intervention was short-lived, however. The Vietnam War split the American foreign policy establishment, a division that continues to this day. For almost twenty years now, U.S. security policy in the developing world has been wandering without a compass, as the stalemate has continued between those who see security threats in the spread of communist ideology and those who distinguish between vital and peripheral interests and measure the threat to both by an opponent's capabilities.

The Failure of the Rio Treaty System

There are, of course, valid reasons why the United States must be sensitive to the ideological orientation of neighboring states. It is not in the security interest of the United States if a neighboring regime's ideology does lead to the concession of military facilities to a hostile great power. Since World War II, the problem for U.S. policy has been to deal with Marxist-Leninist revolutions in the Americas in a way that forecloses the possibility that such movements, if successful, could become strategic assets to the Soviet Union and, at the same time, avoids the political cost that classical U.S. modes of intervention produce. For the most part, the United States has failed the latter test.

Nor has the collective security system created in the 1940s by the Rio Treaty and the OAS Charter met the challenge. The flaw in that system was that it was modeled after the classic alliance, in which states band together in order to combine their strength against a common external threat. The conditions that are necessary for the classic model to function were not present in the inter-American system, however, for two reasons. First, in the modern era the line between external and internal security threats has become blurred, as revolutionary political movements within states seek support from like-minded powers outside. This ambiguity has meant that there has been room for disagreement among the members of the inter-American system as to the origins of a particular internal conflict—indigenous grievances or external subversion—and therefore disagreement over how to deal with it. This problem might not have been fatal had it not been for the fact that in this defensive alliance the leading power had long been accustomed to taking matters into its own hands and thus itself had come to be regarded by the other members as an "external" security threat. In these circumstances, it was difficult, if not impossible, for a truly collegial system to develop. Instead, the process often broke down, as the Latin Americans, viewing the cure as worse than the disease, resisted U.S. solutions that called for intervention.

This history has made the Latin Americans react with extreme suspicion to almost any U.S. proposal for collective action to address a security or political problem in the region. Thus, a vicious circle was created in which the United States, despairing of Latin American cooperation in reacting to what it regarded as security threats, became increasingly unilateralist, and Latin Americans became increasingly reluctant to follow a U.S. lead. Yet, the kinds of problems that the nations of the hemisphere are facing as the century draws to a close demand a collective response. How to change the vicious circle into a virtuous one?

The answer calls for uncharacteristic behavior by the United States. In the face of a political or security problem that is primarily local or regional in origin, the United States should encourage others in the Americas to take the lead in finding solutions. This will not happen, however, if the forum of first resort for addressing such issues is always the Organization of American States. Whatever the reality, the myth that the United States dominates the OAS is too great to be overcome by quiet diplomacy. What is needed is a system in which the response to threats to the peace is decentralized to the lowest level at which action might be effective.

This innovation is not simply for cosmetic purposes. Aside from avoiding the suspicion and tension produced when the United States is thrust into a leadership role, there is an important substantive reason for keeping the United States in the background: if the burden of dealing with the problem were to be placed on the Latin Americans, they would be forced to face the issues giving rise to the crisis in the first place—without being distracted by the issue of U.S. involvement.

If subregional groups were able to resolve the problem, all to the good; if they were not, a more prominent role for the United States might be necessary and the OAS would be the vehicle for reaching an understanding of what should be done. At that stage, however, greater U.S. participation would presumably be actively sought by the Latin Americans and the chances would be greater that they and the North Americans would see the problem in a similar way.

Do the conditions exist for such a system to work? It may appear paradoxical when one considers the low estate to which U.S.-Latin American relations have fallen, but the conditions for a decentralized collective system may be better today than at any time since the 1930s. Collective action requires collective responsibility. The very alienation from the United States produced by U.S. unilateralism in security matters and U.S. neglect of economic issues has led the Latin Americans in recent years to take upon themselves greater responsibility for resolving regional problems. There are a number of examples of this trend toward a collective approach, but the most striking, by far, has been the Contadora group's mediation effort. It is worth pondering the Contadora experience for what it tells us, not about the Central American problem, but about current Latin American attitudes toward intraregional conflict and, therefore, about the prospects for collective security in the future.

The Significance of the Contadora

As Carlos Rico's chapter in this book points out, the Contadora initiative marked a sharp departure from traditional Latin American behavior. Previously, in those intraregional military conflicts that the United States viewed as impinging on its own security, the Latin Americans had confined themselves to a passive role: they were resigned to putting up with U.S. attempts to deal with such crises, however misguided they might view the U.S. approach. The Contadora group, in contrast, took the initiative to deal with a military conflict in an area that the United States had always regarded as vital to its national security and to do so in a way that ran counter to U.S. preferences. The reasons for this change in attitude are complex. Stated briefly, however, they are bound up in the evolution of the international system in the postwar era.[15]

Why did these countries, each of which had powerful incentives not to offend the United States, cross it in this instance? Obviously, they must have felt that important national interests were at stake. It is true that their reasons for becoming involved in the search for a solution to the Central American crisis were not identical.[16] They had, however, one powerful motive in common: the fear that the growing confrontation between the United States and the Sandinistas carried with it the dangers of an escalating military conflict that would have negative repercussions on their own national security.[17]

Traditionally, when the Latin American countries have opposed U.S. policies their opposition has been rhetorical—to criticize U.S. actions, usually in multilateral fora. The Latin Americans have felt that their bilateral interests prevented them from doing more, and, moreover, the United States had the power. However, in this new era, in which political changes are making military power less usable, it turns out that security problems may be an area in which the Latin Americans can do more than simply denounce U.S. intervention. Contadora has demonstrated that it is possible for the Latin Americans to counter U.S. actions that threaten their interests by taking the diplomatic initiative themselves to resolve problems. Some Latin Americans react to this suggestion by charging that this is "doing the Americans' dirty work for them." But this implies that there would be no such problems in the hemisphere but for the United States, which is nonsense.

A multilateral regime will not survive as an effective instrument if it does not have some successes. In this regard, the Contadora experience is instructive in two ways. In the first place, even though none of the draft peace agreements that the group offered to the Central Americans over the course of some four years was adopted by those countries, from the point of view of the members of the Contadora group the effort was successful. It bought time—time in which the political process in the United States prevented the further escalation of the Reagan administration's efforts to overthrow the Sandinista regime by proxy, and time in which the Central Americans themselves, partly because of resentment at the attempts of outsiders to design a settlement, managed to agree on their own formula for stopping the fighting and checking outside intervention.

On the other hand, the failure of the Central American countries to accept a settlement based on the draft Contadora treaties demonstrated that, while the United States may no longer be able to impose a settlement of conflicts in the region, neither can the Latin Americans effect a solution that the United States actively opposes. If collective security in the Americas is to be revitalized, it must be with the collaboration of the United States.

Collective Security: Weighing Costs and Benefits

If the Latin Americans give signs of being ready to assume the burdens of collectively keeping the peace, what about the North Americans? Traditionally, U.S. policymakers have found the costs of multilateralism difficult to bear. The cost is that each member nation must cede some control over the design and execution of policy and action. This requires a disposition to defer to the desires of the majority even while one has some reservations about the wisdom of the course of action preferred by the majority; it requires a willingness to accept what may seem like second-best solutions on the premise of the old saying that "the perfect is the enemy of the good." It places a high value on preserving the unity of the group. It requires less arrogance and more respect for the views of others than North Americans have traditionally displayed in dealing with Latin Americans. Up to now, U.S. leaders have found these costs to be too high, at least in this hemisphere.

Will U.S. leaders be willing to pay those costs in the future? That depends on their cost/benefit analysis when comparing the multilateral route with unilateralism. Certainly the price of unilateral intervention has been great. To take only a recent example, the Reagan administration's intervention in Nicaragua became the most divisive foreign policy issue since the Vietnam War. The effort to shield the intervention from its opponents in the public and the Congress led to the second assault on the Constitution in little more than a decade. The cost has also been high in terms of this country's broader interests in the region. Americans need to ask themselves which poses the greater threat to U.S. national security, the Salvadoran guerrillas or the Colombian drug mafia, Fidel Castro or the destruction of Brazil's rain forests?

Changing the Doctrine

But no cost/benefit analysis will point to sharing responsibility with the Latin Americans for security crises as long as the ideologically driven National Security Doctrine dominates the political debate in the United States. Rico's chapter shows that the Contadora group labored mightily to devise a Central American settlement that would severely limit Nicaragua's capacity to serve as a military asset to the Soviet Union or to threaten its neighbors, only to find that nothing short of the demise of the Sandinista regime would satisfy Washington. A sine qua non of collective security is the acceptance by the United States of Pastor's Indirect Security approach.

For this shift in the dominant paradigm for U.S. security policy toward Latin America, nothing less than presidential leadership will be required. The president must convince the U.S. public that what many will call threats to U.S. security, whether they take the form of radical revolutionaries or drug dealers, can be most effectively dealt with by multilateral cooperation.

This will be no easy task. There are skeptics in both the United States and Latin America about any effort to revive a collective security system in the hemisphere. In the United States, the defenders of unilateralism typically accuse Latin American leaders of hypocrisy. The Latin Americans, it is alleged, will say in private that they would be delighted if the United States would "send in the marines" to crush revolutionaries or narco-dictators, but will not publicly support U.S. intervention because they feel obliged to pander to public opinion. Neither, so the argument goes, will Latin American leaders support collective action to counter a threat to U.S. security, lest they appear to be accomplices of the United States. Hence, say the unilateralists, the United States has no alternative to intervention, and, besides, "our friends" in Latin America do not really object to it anyway.

But this line of reasoning misreads history, which shows that Latin Americans do distinguish between real military threats to U.S. security and ideological or nationalistic anti-Americanism and that they have historically supported collective action to counter the former. This was the case on the eve of World War II and again in the Cuban missile crisis. On the other hand, the majority of Latin Americans are wary of U.S. calls for intervention that appear to be solely aimed at bringing down a regime that, although anti-American, by itself poses no threat to U.S. security.

Convincing North American skeptics that the Latin Americans are not just hypocritical "free riders" is not, however, the most important challenge facing a U.S. president who wants to make a historic shift toward collective security. The key question for all North Americans, skeptics or not, is whether—given the history of differences between us and the Latin Americans about what constitutes a security threat—the protection of vital U.S. national security interests can be compatible with a regional collective security system in which the Latin Americans have real power. This brings us back to the problem of the traditional North American view that regimes that espouse antidemocratic ideologies (as distinct from those that are merely antidemocratic in practice) are per se a threat to U.S. security. This belief has time and again prevented a meeting of the minds with the Latin Americans on security issues. The policy that logically flows from it is to deal with such regimes as if their preferences and their capabilities were identical, i.e., to attempt to destroy them. This the Latin Americans cannot support.

Fortunately, the link between ideology and security that has bedeviled U.S. policy since the end of World War II may at last have been broken. The ideological enemy appears to have decided to drop out of the competition. By adopting perestroika and glasnost, Gorbachev and his followers have virtually admitted the failure of the Marxist-Leninist model. Preoccupied as they are with the herculean task of achieving a peaceful internal revolution, Soviet leaders appear to be ready to make major concessions on security issues and to retrench throughout the Third World. This, in turn, should significantly ease the task of a president who wishes to deal with Latin American revolutionaries as regional problems susceptible to regional solutions rather than as strategic threats.

To be sure, U.S. unilateralists will point to that unreconstructed revolutionary, Fidel Castro, and the evidence that he continues to supply arms to the Salvadoran rebels and probably to Marxist revolutionary movements elsewhere in the region, to argue that the USSR is not ceasing to support revolution in Latin America.

The truthfulness of Moscow's claim that it no longer arms revolutionaries in Latin America and its willingness to bring pressure to bear on Castro to do the same should be possible to determine in time. If the USSR cooperates, then continued intervention by Cuba will clearly be a regional, rather than an East-West, problem.

Latin American willingness to accept the responsibilities of collective security, which, under extreme circumstances, include the possibility of collective intervention, will only be determined in practice. At this point, it is not possible to say whether a collective security system, such as that proposed by Contadora or Esquipulas, will contain the proselytizing ambitions of Castro unless such a system is put into place. What can be said, however, is that the United States and Latin America have the best opportunity since the Good Neighbor Policy of creating an effective collective security system in the Americas. To fail to try to build that system because of the doubts of the skeptics is to engage in a self-fulfilling prophecy; worse, it is irresponsible since the alternative is to fall back on the posture of the last thirty-five years and wait for it to produce another foreign policy crisis like the Contra policy.

What are the ingredients from the U.S. side of a new policy? First, the United States would continue to make it clear that the concession of military facilities to hostile powers or their introduction of weapons into this hemisphere that are threatening to the United States is inadmissible and that the United States will take whatever measures that are necessary to block such adventurism. There is no reason to believe that, in such circumstances, the United States would not be backed up by Latin America and the Caribbean.

Second, the United States would accept, at least implicitly, that the ideological complexion of other governments does not *in itself* affect the vital security interests of the United States. In security questions, a government should be judged more by its actions than by its rhetoric. As Pastor argues earlier in this volume, the U.S. response should be commensurate with the nature of the problem posed by a revolutionary movement or regime. In all instances, it would be essential to have the input of the Latin Americans from the outset both in evaluating the problem and devising a solution. It is a bit strange when Washington is more concerned about security threats to other countries than the governments of those countries are themselves.

This does not mean that the United States should be indifferent to the nature of regimes in the hemisphere, or should turn the other cheek. Like all states, the United States has interests beyond security, including the way a state treats its citizens and its neighbors, not to mention traditional economic and political interests. But these interests can be defended short of seeking to overthrow the offending regime. In most cases, moreover, they can be most effectively defended in concert with other like-minded nations.

Nor does it mean that the United States should leave the Latin Americans entirely to their own devices in dealing with a security problem that has an external dimension, as, for example, when a regime acquires armaments in a quantity and a type that its neighbors see as threatening. In such cases, the United States should be willing to be enlisted by the states concerned to put pressure on external arms suppliers not to support such destabilizing activity. Such efforts will only carry weight if the United States is not providing a convenient excuse for the arms build-up by itself fomenting insurgency.

Latin American Security, Latin American Responsibility

On the Latin American side, it is essential for a successful collective security regime that Latin American governments be willing to confront situations that threaten the peace and security of the region or a subregion. In the future, the threat may come from a revolutionary movement that attempts to spread its system by supporting kindred guerrilla movements elsewhere in the region or it may come from a brutal dictator like a Noriega or a Pinochet. If the Latin American community proclaims that these are rules of international law that binds nations, rules like sovereignty, self-determination, and human rights, it must take some responsibility for enforcing these rules, particularly if the United States is no longer claiming a prerogative to act as policeman.

On this question, the evidence of recent history is mixed. Sandinista Nicaragua had offered a test case of a regime motivated by its ideology to act in ways that its neighbors have regarded as threatening. In this instance, the Latin American community did react. Although it can be argued that the Contadora group was motivated more by its desire to end U.S. intervention than to protect Nicaragua's neighbors, once the mediation was underway the security of the other Central American states inevitably became the focus of the negotiations.

On the other hand, there is Panama. Spokesmen for the Bush administration pointed to the OAS failure to impose sanctions on the Noriega regime to justify its acting unilaterally in Panama. But it must be kept in mind that the Noriega case did not represent a security crisis. Noriega was not attempting to subvert his neighbors, and, in spite of his ties to Cuba, no one suggested that General Noriega was a security problem. What was at issue was his repression of the Panamanian people and his involvement with the drug trade.

Thus, the Noriega case, while not a security problem, did involve the issue of intervention. Latin Americans have traditionally been opposed to any governmental action, multilateral or not, that might be interpreted as interference in another country's internal affairs, particularly its internal politics, for fear that such actions could constitute a precedent for interference in their own country later. It is little wonder that the Latin Americans were wary of going beyond traditional diplomacy to persuade Noriega to leave, all the more so when it could be said with some reason that this was a bilateral conflict between the Panamanian dictator and the United States. Indeed, what was noteworthy about the OAS role in this case was not that it failed to oust Noriega, but that it even tried.

That the Latin Americans were willing to depart, even to the extent they did in the case of Noriega, from their traditional hands-off attitude, was indicative of an important change: the taboo against outside interference in internal political affairs has weakened over the last two decades, as human rights has come to be accepted as a valid international issue. The Inter-American Commission on Human Rights, for example, after an anodyne existence for many years, has since the late 1970s become active in investigating and condemning abuses in OAS member countries. The OAS vote against Noriega indicated that the line between human rights and political rights may now also be fading. The debate in the future may no longer be over nonintervention vs. intervention, but over intervention for which purposes and in what form?

Unfortunately, the Panama invasion can only have the effect of delaying such a change. It will harden the innate Latin American resistance to any collective action that concerns itself with internal affairs, especially if it includes the United States. Nevertheless, those Latin Americans who are unwilling to concede to the inter-American community any right to inject itself into domestic affairs are themselves partly responsible for the unpleasant consequences that may follow. In that respect, the statement of the government of Venezuela on the invasion of Panama was significant. In its comments, that government said that the U.S. military action was in part due to "a lack of an effective and firm response by our countries to the violation of human rights and constitutional norms on the part of the de facto Government of Panama."[18]

As the Panama case shows, the temptations to future intervention need not be new Marxist-Leninist revolutions. Frustration over the inability to stem the flow of drugs into the United States has increasingly given rise to pressure for military solutions, and the successful overthrow of Noriega will reinforce that view. Yet absent the powerful impulse that the postwar marriage of ideology and security has given to intervention, it will be more difficult for U.S. administrations to justify attempts to apply military solutions to problems that are rooted in indigenous economic and social forces. In that sense, Panama, with its peculiar relationship to the United States, may be an aberration, not a harbinger. Confronting the perils of modern interdependence is too urgent to justify turning away from collective responses, no matter how great the provocation to do so.

New Policies, Not New Organizations

The architects of any new effort at collective responsibility for the hemisphere's problems will have to take into account the sensitivities that a hundred years of history have engendered. In particular, any new collective security system will have to be based on a leadership role for Latin America and the Caribbean. The OAS should become a "court of last resort" and defer in the first instance to Latin American and Caribbean institutions and groups that are already in existence. The most promising of these is the Group of Seven, which constitutes the original Contadora Group and its Support Group and which includes all the big and middle powers of the region.

What should be avoided is yet another attempt to "reform" the OAS. There has been almost constant organizational tinkering with the OAS since its inception, with little positive effect. What is required, instead, is as simple as it is rare: acts of statesmanship. The dictionary defines a statesman as a "sagacious, far-sighted politician." Such a leader will intuitively understand that the well-worn ruts of national behavior often travel in vicious circles. He will dare to break with shibboleths that hold men prisoners to the past and will offer a bold vision of a better future. At the same time, statesmanship requires that the new vision be grounded in the possibilities of the present; it must be an idea whose time has come.

There is such a vision. It is of a hemisphere in which responsibility for keeping the peace and security is shared among its nations, rather than being the special burden—and prerogative—of the strongest among them.

Notes

1. A term used by Lloyd C. Gardner. See his "The Evolution of the Interventionist Impulse," in *Intervention in the 1980s: U.S. Foreign Policy in the Third World,* ed. Peter J. Schraeder (Boulder/London: Lynne Rienner Publishers, 1989), Chapter 2.

2. See Chapter 1 in this book.

3. Sources: Inter-American Development Bank, *Annual Report, 1988*, pp. 114-115, and Rudiger Dornbusch, "Reducing Transfers from Debtor Countries" (paper delivered at the Second Harvard Conference on New Initiatives on Latin American Debt, May 15-16, 1989), pp. 13-14.

4. Quoted in Dexter Perkins, *A History of the Monroe Doctrine* (Boston: Little, Brown, 1941), p. 175.

5. Stanley Hoffmann, "The Political Ethics of International Relations," Seventh Morgenthau Memorial Lecture on Ethics and Foreign Policy (New York: Carnegie Council on Ethics and International Affairs, 1988, pamphlet) p. 9.

6. For a history of U.S. foreign relations in this period, see Samuel Flagg Bemis, *A Diplomatic History of the United States* (New York: Henry Holt & Co., 1936), Chapters 5-12.

7. See Domínguez's discussion of the ideological content of the Monroe Doctrine in Chapter 3, pp. 82-91. Domínguez also points out the striking parallelism between the language of the Monroe Doctrine and the resolution approved one hundred and thirty-one years later by the Organization of American States at the urging of Secretary of State John Foster Dulles.

8. In his annual message to Congress of December 2, 1845, Polk referred to the Monroe Doctrine "as our settled policy, that no future European colony or dominion shall, with our consent, be planted or established on any part of the North American continent." [Cited in Dexter Perkins, *The Monroe Doctrine, 1826-1867* (Baltimore: Johns Hopkins Press, 1933), p. 89]. This revival of the doctrine was prompted by British and French diplomatic efforts to thwart the annexation of Texas by the United States and British intrigues in California designed to prevent U.S. acquisition of that territory, over which Mexico exercised a tenuous sovereignty. Three years later, during the War with Mexico, Polk again invoked the Monroe Doctrine in reference to attempts by an autonomous faction then in power in the Yucutan to annex the territory to Spain or Great Britain, as well as to the United States (Perkins, pp. 171-192). Perkins states that this declaration of Polk went beyond Monroe's prohibition and denied the right of a people in the Americas to voluntarily transfer their allegiance to a European power. Perkins says that Polk's declaration was "the beginning of that historic process by which a principle of non-intervention has been transferred into a principle of intervention." (Perkins, pp. 175-176).

9. Cole Blasier, *The Hovering Giant: U.S. Responses to Revolutionary Change in Latin America, 1910-1985*, rev. ed., (Pittsburgh: University of Pittsburgh Press, 1985), pp.106-107.

10. For a treatment of this period, see Bryce Wood, *The Making of the Good Neighbor Policy* (New York: Columbia University Press, 1961), esp. Introduction and Chapter 15.

11. See Chapter 4 in this volume.

12. See Pastor's critique of the "direct" version of the National Security Perspective in Chapter 4 of this book.

13. For the identity of the American nationality with American political ideas and institutions, see Samuel P. Huntington, *American Politics: The Promise of Disharmony* (Cambridge, Mass: Belknap Press, 1981), Chapter 2, pp. 13-30.

14. For the story of how the advocates of a global commitment to containment of the Soviet Union came to dominate the National Security debate in the Truman administration and the ways in which successive administrations attempted to reconcile unlimited commitments with limited resources, see John Lewis Gaddis, *Strategies of Containment* (New York, Oxford: Oxford University Press, 1982). For an excellent description and critique of the doctrine of universal vulnerability and the

seamless web of U.S. security interests, see Bruce W. Jentleson, "American Commitments in the Third World: Theory vs. Practice", *International Organization* 41, no. 4 (Autumn 1987): 667-704.

15. Chapter 6 in this book.

16. See Susan Kaufman Purcell, "Demystifying Contadora," *Foreign Affairs* 64, no. 1, (Fall 1985).

17. Chapter 6 in this book.

18. *New York Times,* December 21, 1989

"Collective Security in the Americas: New Directions," Statement of an Inter-American Working Group, June 1988

A Continent at Risk

The security of Latin America and the Caribbean is today at risk. Huge external debt, deep economic depression, and pervasive inequities threaten the social fabric and political cohesion of many countries. Insurgencies, civil wars, and external interventions cripple much of Central America and the Andean region of South America. The trade in narcotics has become a deadly plague that destroys thousands of lives and threatens the integrity of the state itself. Terrorism, by governments as well as by their enemies, is a scourge in a number of countries. Massive migration—people fleeing repression or hardship—strains the capacity of receiving nations to cope.

These and other challenges cry out for close cooperation among the countries of the Americas. Domestic and international trends throughout the hemisphere, particularly the region-wide turn toward democracy, make inter-American cooperation more feasible than at any time in the past generation. But it is also painfully evident that the procedures for inter-American cooperation created after World War II have all but collapsed. Nowhere is that collapse more evident than in the security area. In the crisis that has gripped Central America since 1980, the Organization of American States has been virtually irrelevant.

This disturbing paradox—increasing and more complex threats to the hemisphere's security, enhanced readiness for collective action, and yet the atrophy of existing collective procedures—has motivated our working group.

It brought us together in the first instance, and it has convinced us to persist even though differences in perceptions, judgments, and priorities made it difficult for us to forge agreement. Our members come from countries that range from the largest to some of the least powerful. We include individuals from diverse parties and tendencies in the United States, Latin America and the Caribbean. Several of us have served in governments or in regional institutions; others have worked in business or academia. However, all of us have participated actively—either as scholars or practitioners—in our nations' foreign policies. We still differ on many issues.

None of us necessarily agrees with every sentence in this report. But we all affirm that this document reflects our group's consensus, reached after four extended discussions over the last two years.

All of us believe that the countries of the Americas can, should—indeed must—work together more effectively to achieve peace and security. We know that doing so will not be easy, for distrust and division between the United States and Latin America have deepened in recent years. But we believe that the time has come to construct a new framework to help protect the security of the peoples of the hemisphere.

The Central American Tragedy and the Future

The Central American crisis of the 1980s has brought into sharp relief the absence of functioning collective responses to threats to regional peace and security. The Central American wars have expanded and intensified, killing many thousands of people, displacing hundreds of thousands into other nations, and destroying a generation's progress toward economic development. Arms races have escalated, military forces have expanded, foreign interventions have increased, wars have spilled over borders—and still the hemisphere's collective security procedures have gone unused.

We dare to hope, though we are far from sure, that the Central American crisis may now be on the way to resolution, primarily on the basis of diplomatic efforts undertaken in the Central American countries themselves. But even if the brutal violence in Central America can be stopped, the hemisphere must do more to prevent such a tragedy from happening again.

Events in Central America have demonstrated that unilateral military intervention—direct or indirect—is not the answer to such conflicts. Whatever its motives, such intervention is widely reflected throughout the hemisphere—increasingly within the United States as well as in Latin America. It is no longer a politically sustainable means of dealing with conflicts in which the security threat is incipient or unclear. Some rejoice at the constraints on intervention, others lament them—but it is important for all to face their limitations. With unilateral intervention bankrupt, and with established collective security procedures rendered impotent, the Western Hemisphere is in danger of lacking any effective means of dealing with threats to regional security. This dangerous vacuum prompts our shared concern.

Cause for Hope

In spite of the current disarray, we believe that a new approach to security problems in the Americas is feasible if our leaders take the initiative. We see at least four developments in recent years that could provide the basis for enhanced collective action, with new forms and emphases:

1. There is a new consciousness in all our countries that many of the urgent problems that confront our societies cannot be resolved within national boundaries. This change is particularly notable in the United States. While Latin Americans have long been keenly aware of the vulnerability of their societies to events abroad, the U.S. public is only now coming to realize that developments in Latin America can have an important impact on their welfare. The next step is for political leaders to convert this awareness of our mutual interdependence into support for cooperation on a wide range of issues.

2. In the past, the imbalance of power between the United States and Latin America discouraged Latin American states from taking the initiative on those regional security issues to which the United States accorded a high priority. In the 1980s, that has changed. No longer is Latin America resigned to letting the United States define threats to hemispheric security and to acquiescing in U.S. policies to cope with them. The Contadora initiative and the Arias plan are an indication of Latin American willingness to take responsibility to solve security crises. The Contadora mediation effort ultimately involved eight Latin American countries, including the six largest. It brought to bear the combined moral authority of the rest of Latin America on the parties of the Central American conflict to try to reach a peaceful settlement. It laid the groundwork for the August 1987 agreement among the five Central American countries that has created a framework for achieving peace.

3. At the same time, the Contadora experience has demonstrated that it is difficult for such Latin American efforts to succeed in the face of U.S. opposition, just as U.S. attempts to resolve these problems are unlikely to prosper without Latin American cooperation. Security in the Americas today requires the joint efforts of both the United States and Latin America.

4. Latin Americans and North Americans increasingly agree that they have a shared interest in the fate of democracy in the hemisphere. In the past, Latin Americans have been wary lest efforts to promote a political system, including democracy, lead to intervention. Against this background, it is notable that the draft Contadora Agreement and the Central American Peace Accord (also known as Esquipulas II) both include commitments to take specific steps toward political pluralism and the protection of civil and human rights. This is a significant change. In the United States, by the same token, there is a growing awareness that a functioning democracy that promotes economic growth and social justice is not only desirable in itself but is the best assurance against the rise of the Marxist-Leninist regimes—regimes that are hostile to the United States and may provide an opportunity for Soviet intrusion.

Fundamental Principles of Policy

Four basic principles are fundamental if an effort to create a new framework of regional cooperation on security is to succeed:

(1) Collective action to resolve regional security crises should be the guiding principle of each nation's policy in the Americas.

No nation will forswear unilateral action if it believes its vital national interests are in immediate jeopardy. But too often unilateral action in this hemisphere has been unwarranted and its costs have been excessive. In 1947, the United States joined with the Latin American nations to establish a collective security arrangement for the Americas. A pillar of that agreement was a pledge by all the parties not to intervene unilaterally. Since the Rio Treaty was signed, the United States has resorted on a number of occasions to military or paramilitary intervention in Latin America, asserting reasons of national security. One result has been to vitiate the very collective security system that was supposed, among other objectives, to prevent extracontinental intervention in this hemisphere.

In recent years, the undeniable result of unilateral intervention has been to divide U.S. public opinion deeply. A foreign policy that arouses such broad and intense domestic opposition is ultimately unsustainable.

For the Latin American nations, the commitment of the United States to nonintervention was a major motive for their adherence to the Rio Pact. Nevertheless, over the years a number of Latin American nations have themselves intervened in the affairs of their neighbors by aiding insurrections. These actions have also weakened the general principle of nonintervention which Latin America has long espoused.

In those instances in which there was an agreement between the governments of Latin America and the United States on the nature of a security threat, collective action was taken; examples are the attempted invasions of Costa Rica from Nicaragua in 1948 and 1955, the sanctions against the Trujillo regime for its attempted subversion in Venezuela (1960), the sanctions against Cuba in the 1960s prompted by its fomenting of guerrilla activity in several countries, Latin American support in the OAS for the U.S. blockade during the Cuban missile crisis of 1962, and the peacekeeping mission in the El Salvador-Honduras war (1969).

For both the United States and Latin America, confronting security problems collectively is the best course. For the United States, in the case of a clear and present danger to its vital security interests, it will almost certainly find that the situation is also perceived by Latin America as a clear and present danger to Hemispheric security, as in the missile crisis of 1962. In ambiguous cases, such as an internal revolution, the degree of the security threat, if any, may be interpreted differently by various nations. In these instances, a collective appraisal of the situation is more likely to result in an appropriate Hemispheric response. A policy that has been agreed upon between the United States and Latin America will have international legitimacy and the backing of the U.S. public. Such a policy is more likely to be sustainable over the long run. Also, by isolating or otherwise sanctioning the nations contributing to the crisis, multilateral actions are likely to be more effective than unilateral measures in dealing with the security problem.

For Latin America, an important motive historically for joining in a collective security arrangement with the United States has been to check U.S. impulses toward unilateral intervention. In the future, however, as Latin America increasingly assumes more responsibility for regional security, a challenge will be to secure the constructive involvement of the United States in keeping or restoring the peace.

(2) The United States and Latin America must recognize that they have different security priorities and concerns, that these differences must be accepted as legitimate, and that they should make efforts to reconcile them through multilateral consultation and collective action.

As a global power, the United States sees its security interests in Latin America largely in terms of its worldwide concerns. It looks at political developments in the region in the light of their potential effect on the global power balance. The United States is especially sensitive to the possibility of Soviet power expanding in the Caribbean Basin.

The Latin American nations see their security interests in a different way. A number are concerned with the security of their borders, some of which are still in dispute, and the effective exercise of sovereignty over all the national territory, which is often tenuous because of underdevelopment. They fear interference in their affairs by others, and the United States at times has been regarded as the greatest threat in this respect.

Most importantly, the majority of the countries of the region have acute social problems, stemming from poverty, social and economic inequality, economic stagnation and unemployment. Political institutions are often fragile. In these conditions, a high rate of economic growth and social transformation are essential to national security. For this reason, the Latin Americans see their security as most directly threatened by massive foreign debts, protectionism in the industrialized countries, and external economic shocks from the international economy.

Because of these differing perspectives, internal changes in the region, especially revolutionary changes, are perceived by Latin American countries and the United States in different ways. Many in the United States see revolutionary change as led by Marxist-Leninists who are hostile to the United States and who, it is believed, are likely to align their country with the Soviet Union, thus posing a threat to U.S. security. Most Latin Americans, regardless of how they feel about revolution, do not see it as constituting a direct threat to the security of the United States and therefore do not agree that U.S. intervention is an appropriate response. While many Latin Americans regard revolution as a threat to their own nation's security, they usually see revolution as arising primarily from domestic causes and as requiring essentially domestic solutions, rather than as mainly externally inspired and driven. These differences of perception between Latin America and the United States have made it difficult to agree on collective measures to deal with revolution in the hemisphere. If they are to be reconciled, both sides need to adopt a new approach that takes account of the legitimate concerns of the other.

(3) If conflicts over how to deal with security crises are to be minimized and resolved, the United States must make a clearer distinction than it has heretofore between its vital security interests and its other interests in the region.

In regard to vital security interests—for example, when there is an indication that the Soviet Union may be contemplating the acquisition of military facilities or the introduction of weapons into the Western Hemisphere that the United States would view as threatening—the United States should deal directly with the Soviet Union and the other country involved. In such cases, it should be able to count on the backing of Latin America and the Caribbean, whose interests would be ill-served by the expansion of Soviet military power in the region. Indeed, Latin American concern about the intrusion of a Soviet military presence was demonstrated by the Contadora group's Statement of Twenty-One Principles and draft treaties, which call for the reciprocal elimination or reduction of the foreign military and security presence in Central America.

The political or ideological complexion of a Latin American government does not *in itself* affect the vital security interests of the United States. With respect to revolutionary movements or regimes that may have other ties to the Soviet Union—short of a significant Soviet military role—the threat to U.S. security interests will be at most indirect. If a revolutionary regime in a Latin American country poses a security threat to its neighbors through aggression or subversion, it would be at least as great a concern to the rest of Latin America as to the United States, and the United States should first look to the Latin American states for leadership on how to deal with the problem. In this way, the response of the United States and of Latin America to such challenges is more likely to be proportional to the nature of the threat and more effective than it has been in the past.

(4) For their part, the countries of Latin America and the Caribbean must be prepared to take collective measures to counter acts of aggression or

subversion by one state against another.

Until recently, Latin American nations have often been reluctant to involve themselves in resolving conflicts elsewhere in the region, largely because of their adherence to the principle of nonintervention. Yet it is precisely such conflicts that can draw in other countries and become security problems for the entire area. The more quickly the Latin American and Caribbean nations can act to contain such conflicts, the less likely that outside powers will be drawn in. Collective initiative by Latin America and the Caribbean to deal with security crises in the region is the best guarantee against unilateral intervention—by the United States or any other nation. The Contadora initiative and the Central American Peace Accord reflected recognition of this fact and are significant precedents.

A New Security Framework

If the foregoing principles are translated into policy, the initiatives taken by a number of Latin American and Caribbean countries in recent years to deal collectively with regional security issues could become the building blocks of a new inter-American collective security system—a set of interlocking subregional and regional groupings. Such decentralization is desirable because those countries closest to the problem are more likely to understand its nature and fashion an appropriate response. Subregional organizations and arrangements such as the Central American Peace Accord, the Organization of Eastern Caribbean States, the CARICOM, and the Andean Pact should be the primary vehicles for the resolution of subregional or local security problems. Larger organizations should come into play only upon request of countries in the subregion, or when subregional bodies are not suitable or have proven ineffective.

In this sense, the agreement reached by the Central American nations in Esquipulas, Guatemala in August 1987, which grew out of the initiative of President Arias of Costa Rica and built on the prior efforts of the Contadora Group, may prove to be an example of one way subregional security problems should be handled in the future. The Esquipulas II Accord requires the Central American nations themselves to carry out its provisions but it also calls upon nations from outside Central America to cooperate in its implementation.

At a broader regional level, the members of the Contadora Group and the Support Group—the Group of Eight—have agreed to institutionalize their efforts by having their Chiefs of State and Foreign Ministers meet periodically to coordinate policies on political cooperation, regional integration, external vulnerability and other issues, including security questions. The Group of Eight, in its role as the Contadora and Support

Group, should also continue to assist the Central American countries to reach agreement on other aspects of the region's crisis, such as the stalled negotiations on the issues of arms control, military force levels, and external military support.

The Group of Eight should also take the initiative to deal with future conflicts that arise within Latin America and that threaten to impinge on regional security, when these do not fall under the purview of an existing subregional mechanism, such as the Esquipulas II Accord, or when the Organization of American States is not in the first instance an appropriate venue for their resolution. In such cases, the Group of Eight should seek—and should expect to receive—the cooperation of the United States.

Collective action by these new subregional and regional groups may take several forms. Such action can be undertaken by a group of nations on an ad hoc basis to deal with a specific problem (as was the case with the Contadora Group), or, at the other extreme, it can be carried out by a formally constituted international organization with a body of norms, rules and procedures to which the members have adhered through a treaty or otherwise. Collective action can range from good offices and mediation through economic, political, and, ultimately, military sanctions. To date, Latin American initiatives in security crises have been confined to good offices and mediation. In that sense, they do not constitute a fully developed collective security system. That is no reason, however, to denigrate the importance and usefulness of these regional and subregional groups, and they should be encouraged to develop their capabilities in the collective security field.

The Latin American countries have long aspired to reaching agreements on arms control that would reduce the threat of war among themselves and help maintain the region's traditionally low level of military expenditure. The Group of Eight or an extension of it should revive regional and subregional arms control discussions.

The majority of countries in the Caribbean archipelago have achieved independence only in the past three decades; most have joined the Organization of American States but have not signed the Rio Treaty. These countries, many of which are extremely small and possess limited capabilities, are in the process of consolidating their sovereignty. Consultation with them is required to ensure that they have a meaningful place in the systems of collective security of the hemisphere and that existing hemispheric institutions adapt their structures to cope with the particular concerns of these countries. In addition, the Caribbean Community should be encouraged to strengthen its relationship with the Dominican Republic and Haiti.

Latin American and Caribbean efforts to deal with security problems will be more likely to succeed if they have the cooperation of the United States. A link between Latin American and Caribbean security arrangement and the

United States continues to be needed. An institutional link already exists in the Organization of American States, but only on paper. Adoption of the policies we recommend should lead to reinvigorated inter-American security arrangements, which in turn, should enable the OAS to function effectively in the security field.

Looking to the Future

The Latin American democracies and the United States should act on their common perception that democracy is essential to the preservation of individual freedom and the achievement of social justice, which are the twin pillars of peace and security. They should cooperate closely among themselves to encourage democracy in the hemisphere. Such cooperation should take several forms. The chiefs of state should consult regularly with one another about how to strengthen democracy in the region. They should seek a common policy toward dictatorial regimes, especially on such issues as whether to supply weapons and military equipment and when and how to provide economic assistance, both bilateral and multilateral. They should not hesitate to condemn repression in another American state. They should give strong support to the work of the Inter-American Human Rights Commission. Political parties, trade unions, foundations, business groups and other private organizations should increase their support to their counterparts in countries where the infrastructure of democracy needs to be strengthened.

The severe economic crisis of recent years continues to erode the living standards of the peoples of Latin America and the Caribbean. It is a grave threat to the region's security. The transfer of vast resources out of the region to service its foreign debt is a major obstacle to ending the crisis and resuming sustained economic expansion. The United States, as a leader of the creditor nations, should give a high priority to helping the Latin American and Caribbean countries solve the debt crisis. It makes no sense to be concerned about preventing internal instability and conflict in the nations of the region and yet at the same time to ask the debtor countries to take severe austerity measures that aggravate domestic tensions and erode the legitimacy of democratic governments that are forced to carry them out.

In the future, threats to our nations' security will take new forms. Today we see entire nations held hostage by ruthless crime syndicates; tomorrow it may be the destruction of the environment that poses the greatest threat to the hemisphere's security. National security is broader than just military strength. Ultimately, it is based on political freedom, social justice, and economic progress. No nation can ever be totally secure. But mutual recognition in the Americas that each of our nations is vulnerable—and not only to arms—can help us work together to enhance the security of all.

The undersigned agree that the above statement represents their consensus. However, it should be understood that they do not necessarily agree with every sentence in the statement and that they sign it in their personal capacities and not as representatives of the governments or institutions with which they are affiliated.

Peter D. Bell
Richard J. Bloomfield
Oscar Camilión
Jorge I. Domínguez
Mariano Grondona
Jane Jaquette
Milton Katz
James R. Kurth
Vaughan Lewis
Abraham Lowenthal
Ricardo Luna
Francis J. McNeil

Heraldo Muñoz
Daniel Oduber
Robert A. Pastor
Marcial Pérez Chiriboga
Teodoro Petkoff
Susan Kaufman Purcell
David Ronfeldt
Daniel Sharp
Gregory F. Treverton
Richard Ullman
Viron P. Vaky

Individual Statements

Heraldo Muñoz:

If peace and collective security arrangements are to succeed in the hemisphere, the security interests of Latin America as well as those of the United States must be effectively safeguarded and promoted. Collective security must give assurances to all sides involved.

Since intervention by the United States has been viewed as a threat to Latin American security, there is evidently a need for Washington not only to refrain from such unilateral acts in the region but also to disengage from present interventionism, both overt and covert. In the same perspective, the United States cannot expect Latin American countries to actively oppose extracontinental and intraregional security threats while, at the same time, accepting a U.S. military presence in Latin America. Such a position would be highly unrealistic and it would be unacceptable to most Latin Americans. Therefore, it is in the interest of Latin America, and of hemispheric peace and security, to eliminate from the region all external military presence, including that of the United States.

Susan Kaufman Purcell:

A revolutionary regime in a Latin American country that poses a security threat to its neighbors through aggression or subversion might, as this report states, be at least as great a concern to the rest of Latin America as to the United States. This does not mean, however, that these Latin American countries would be willing or able to take effective action against the aggressor country. There are political and other costs that Latin American governments pay if they side with the United States against a fellow Latin American country. At the same time, Latin American governments assume that if there is really a threat to United States security interests by a hostile Marxist guerrilla movement or government in the hemisphere, the United States can and will take care of it unilaterally. This allows the Latin American governments to avoid the political costs of siding with the United States against a Latin American insurgency or hostile government, while simultaneously reaping the political benefits of opposing unilateral intervention by the United States.

The report also notes that Latin American countries at times regard the United States as the greatest threat to hemispheric security. One manifestation of this is their tendency to criticize United States intervention, very broadly defined, in the internal affairs of Latin American countries, such as Cuba, in the region. There cannot be a workable system of collective security in the hemisphere as long as such a double standard continues to operate.

Selected Bibliography

Atkins, G. Pope. *Latin America in the International Political System*. Second edition. Boulder: Westview Press, 1989.

Bemis, Samuel Flagg. *A Diplomatic History of the United States*. New York: Henry Holt & Co., 1936.

Blaiser, Cole. *The Giant's Rival: The USSR and Latin America*. Revised Edition. Pittsburgh: University of Pittsburgh Press, 1989.

————. *The Hovering Giant: U.S. Responses to Revolutionary Change in Latin America*. Revised Edition. Pittsburgh: University of Pittsburgh Press, 1985.

Fagen, Richard. *Forging Peace: The Challenge of Central America*. Cambridge, Mass.: Blackwell, 1987.

Farer, Tom J., ed. *The Future of the Inter-American System*. New York: Praeger, 1979.

Gaddis, John Lewis. *Strategies of Containment*. New York, Oxford: Oxford University Press, 1982.

Kissinger, Henry. *Report of the National Bipartisan Commission on Central America*. U.S. Government Printing Office, 1984.

Lowenthal, Abraham F. *Partners in Conflict: The United States and Latin America*. Baltimore: Johns Hopkins University Press, 1987.

Middlebrook, Kevin J. and Carlos Rico, eds. *The United States and Latin America in the 1980s*. Pittsburgh: University of Pittsburgh Press, 1986.

Muñoz, Heraldo. "Is U.S. Foreign Policy its Own Worst Enemy?" *Hemisphere*, vol. I, no. 1, Fall 1988.

———— and Joseph Tulchin, eds. *Latin American Nations in World Politics*. Boulder: Westview Press, 1984.

———— and Robert Wesson, eds. *Latin American Views of U.S. Policy*. New York: Praeger, 1986.

Pastor, Robert A. *Condemned to Repetition: The United States and Nicaragua*. Princeton: Princeton University Press, 1987.

————, ed. *Democracy in the Americas: Stopping the Pendulum*. New York: Holmes and Meier, 1989.

———— and Jorge G. Castañeda, eds. *Limits to Friendship: The United States and Mexico*. New York: Vintage Books, 1988.

Perkins, Dexter. *A History of the Monroe Doctrine*. Boston: Little, Brown, 1941.

Ronfeldt, David. *Geopolitics, Security, and U.S. Strategy in the Caribbean Basin*. F-2997-AF/RC. Rand Corporation, 1983.

Scheman, L. Ronald. *The Inter-American Dilemma*. New York: Praeger, 1988.

Schoultz, Lars. *National Security and United States Policy toward Latin America*. Princeton: Princeton University Press, 1987.

Wood, Bryce. *The Dismantling of the Good Neighbor Policy.* Austin: University of Texas Press, 1985.

————. *The Making of the Good Neighbor Policy.* New York: Columbia University Press, 1961.

Vaky, Viron. "Positive Containment in Nicaragua." *Foreign Policy,* no. 68, Fall 1987.

————, ed. *Governance in the Western Hemisphere.* New York: Praeger, 1983.

Varas, Augusto, ed. *Hemispheric Security and U.S. Policy in Latin America.* Boulder: Westview Press, 1989.

The Contributors

Richard J. Bloomfield, executive director of the World Peace Foundation; former career diplomat: Ambassador to Ecuador, 1976-1978; Ambassador to Portugal, 1978-1982.

Jorge I. Domínguez, professor of government, Harvard University; member, Inter-American Dialogue; former president, Latin American Studies Association.

James R. Kurth, professor of political science, Swarthmore College; professor, Department of Strategy, U.S. Naval War College, 1983-1985; former member, Institute for Advanced Study, Princeton.

Heraldo Muñoz, Ambassador permanent representative of Chile to the Organization of American States; former director, Latin American Foreign Policies Program, Academia de Humanismo Cristiano, Chile; former secretary of international relations, Socialist Party of Chile; president of the Santiago Region, Party for Democracy (PPD).

Robert A. Pastor, professor of political science, Emory University, and director of the Latin American and Caribbean Program at Emory's Carter Center; director of Latin American Affairs of the National Security Council, 1977-1981; author of *Condemned to Repetition: The United States and Nicaragua* and co-author of *Limits to Friendship: The United States and Mexico*.

Marcial Pérez Chiriboga, partner, Baumeister & Brewer, Caracas; Venezuelan Ambassador to the United States 1979-1984; former director, International Policy, Ministry of Foreign Affairs, Venezuela.

Carlos Rico F., professor and senior reseacher, Colegio de Mexico and advisor to the Mexican Foreign Ministry; founder and former director of the Instituto de Estudios de Estados Unidos.

Gregory F. Treverton, senior fellow and director of the European Program, Council on Foreign Relations, New York; senior research associate, Center for Science and International Affairs, Harvard University, 1984-1988; lead consultant on security issues, National Bipartisan Commission on Central America, 1983-1984.

Index

153

About the Book

In the 1980s, events in Central America brought the issue of intervention to the forefront of U.S.-Latin American relations. U.S. support for the contra rebels became not only a major source of friction between Washington and Latin capitals, but, within the United States, the most divisive foreign policy issue since the Vietnam War.

This book explores the underlying causes of U.S. intervention in Latin America and the Caribbean and assesses the prospects for an alternative: a new collective security arrangement that would satisfy the security needs of both the United States and the Latin American and Caribbean countries. The authors examine why the security system established after World War II failed to put an end to unilateral intervention, why the United States and Latin Amnerican nations respond differently to radical revolutions in the region, and the obstacles to and opportunities for a new effort at collective security in the western hemisphere.